MARCHING
to DIFFERENT
DRUMMERS

2nd Edition

Pat Burke Guild & Stephen Garger

Association for Supervision and Curriculum Development
Alexandria, Virginia USA

Association for Supervision and Curriculum Development
1703 N. Beauregard St. • Alexandria, VA 22311-1714 USA
Telephone: 1-800-933-2723 or 703-578-9600 • Fax: 703-575-5400
Web site: http://www.ascd.org • E-mail: member@ascd.org

Gene R. Carter, *Executive Director*
Michelle Terry, *Associate Executive Director, Program Development*
Nancy Modrak, *Director, Publishing*
John O'Neil, *Director of Acquisitions*
Julie Houtz, *Managing Editor of Books*
Jo Ann Irick Jones, *Senior Associate Editor*
René Bahrenfuss, *Copy Editor*
Deborah Whitley, *Proofreader*
Charles D. Halverson, *Project Assistant*

Gary Bloom, *Director, Design and Production Services*
Karen Monaco, *Senior Designer*
Tracey A. Smith, *Production Manager*
Dina Murray, *Production Coordinator*
John Franklin, *Production Coordinator*
Barton Matheson Willse & Worthington, *Desktop Publisher*
Sarah Allen Smith, *Indexer*

Printed in the United States of America.

s11/98

ASCD Stock No. 198186   ASCD member price: $14.95   nonmember price: $17.95

Library of Congress Cataloging-in-Publication Data
Guild, Pat Burke.
    Marching to different drummers / Pat Burke Guild & Stephen Garger. — 2nd ed.
        p.   cm.
    Includes bibliographical references and index.
    ISBN 1-87120-306-5 - (p.bk.)
    1. Learning.   2. Cognition in children.   3. Individualized instruction.   I. Garger, Stephen.
    II. Title.
    LB1060.G85   1998
    370.15'2—ddc21   98-25532
                                                                                         CIP

02 01 00 99 98   5 4 3 2 1

Marching to
Different Drummers

Acknowledgments

I have deep admiration for the dedicated and talented teachers who have showed me how accommodating learning styles can help all students be successful learners. My personal gratitude for inspiration and ideas to Kathi Hand and Loanna Day; for professional support to Dee St. George, Sandy Chock-Eng, and Donna Kehle; and for patience and love to Darren and Sue Anne Guild.

PAT GUILD, JULY 1998

I'd like to thank all the students I have worked with. They heartened me, corrected false impressions, and deepened my knowledge of styles past anything that could be learned from academic research. On a more personal note I'd like to thank my lifelong friend Joseph Dowicyan, who stands by me; my sister Liz Garger, whom I admire more than she knows; my colleague Vanessa Zerillo, for her wise and generous heart; and Margaret Affinito, who inspires me.

STEVE GARGER, JULY 1998

Introduction

If a man does not keep pace with his companions, perhaps it is because he hears a different drummer. Let him step to the music which he hears, however measured or far away.

—HENRY DAVID THOREAU

Do you search for a five-cent error in your checkbook? Why? Some people say they enjoy the challenge of balancing their checkbooks exactly. Some believe the job isn't done until an exact balance is figured. Others want to find the nickel before the error escalates.

Then there are those who have forgotten the last time they balanced their checkbook—or even looked at the balance statement from the bank. They wonder why anyone would waste time searching for such a small error. They know that keeping a checkbook is necessary, but they don't spend any more time with it than required.

And, of course, many people are in between these extremes. They may search for a five-dollar error, but they'll write off a nickel.

Why do people vary in their approaches to such a task? Why do some people say that "you're supposed to balance your checkbook exactly," or "it's the right thing to do," while others deride it as "compulsiveness" and "perfectionism"? Do we learn these behaviors from our parents? If so, how do we explain that siblings often handle their checkbooks differently? Why would someone balance the checkbook for an organization with care and accuracy, yet be casual about a personal account? And why does the "math whiz" not balance his personal checkbook when obviously it's an easy task?

1

A natural response to all these questions is that people are different—fundamentally different in what they care about and what they will spend time doing. Though this is basic common sense, it has tremendous implications for educators.

Individual Differences in Education

Individual differences have intrigued and challenged educators for centuries. On the one hand, the understanding and application of this concept motivates our profession. On the other hand, practical responses to individual differences have almost entirely eluded us. Educator Nathaniel Cantor (1946/1972) identified this dilemma more than 50 years ago: "That there are individual differences in learning has been recognized in theory as often as it has been denied in practice" (p. 185).

This book is based on the belief that each person is unique. In it, we describe a variety of ways people differ, and, in particular, focus on differences in personality traits defined as "style." We address why and how these differences are important for education.

The styles addressed in this book have been labeled variously as learning style, cognitive style, multiple intelligences, teaching style, leadership style, and psychological type. While the names differ, many of the basic concepts are similar, and we have chosen to address them as related topics.

Does balancing a checkbook affect people in education? Perhaps not directly, but if the reason for handling the checkbook in a certain way reveals a basic aspect of personality, then that trait will often be reflected in learning, teaching, or administration. There is an important difference, for example, when one teacher thinks that a creative writing assignment should be neatly typed with correct spelling while another values a free flow of ideas in which errors can be corrected later. In turn, a "perfect paper" is important to some students, but "getting the job done" is good enough for others. Some administrators may base their evaluations on completion of the textbook, but that fact won't matter to others. If some parents believe that schools should prepare students for work and others want schools to provide a "liberal arts" education, their basic differences will be acted out in a budget vote for a music and arts program.

These are only a few examples of how individual differences are reflected in all aspects of education.

Our experiences in studying styles, applying research on styles, teaching about styles, and listening to students and fellow educators talk about styles lead us to believe that style is the most important concept to demand educators' attention in many years. Style is at the core of what it means to be a person. While the concept has been explored for centuries, the past three decades have seen it infused with new energy and direction. Style is essential to any educator's philosophy of education. It touches on classroom practice, administration, and curriculum development. It relates to staff development and to students' study habits. It helps us to understand ourselves and to trust that all students can learn. Perhaps most important, it calls upon educators to recognize actively that people are different. These differences inevitably surface when people learn, teach, supervise, and develop programs.

"Differences in our schools will always exist," a principal observed, "because teachers and students are people, and a fundamental characteristic of people is diversity." Then he decided to view this fact in a positive light: "I have often found it possible to transform differences among children, teachers, parents, and administrators into powerful educational assets" (Barth, 1980, pp. 15 and xvii).

Fundamental personality differences do have the potential to bring diverse talents to education. But if these differences are treated superficially, we will certainly miss many rich opportunities to make the most of these diverse perspectives.

This Book's Scope

This book explores differences in style to help educators better fulfill their responsibilities and experience the joys of helping people realize their potential. It is intended for all practicing educators. Teachers will recognize its messages about themselves and their students, and they should benefit from the practical classroom suggestions. Administrators should find the information relevant to all aspects of their jobs and the suggestions immediately applicable to their work as instructional leaders. Curriculum specialists should be able to use the philosophical framework as well as the direct suggestions. University and college instructors should find the synthesis of complex concepts useful for introducing style to their students. And parents can apply the messages about diversity and support to their own children.

Though we have a wealth of research on style, summaries of these theories and ideas are not easily accessible. This book bridges that gap, describing major research contributions and identifying common themes. We present a summary of concepts, but we do not strive to create one synergistic definition from the different approaches to style.

For those relatively new to the theory of style, we offer basic definitions and examples. Those generally familiar with the concepts should find food for thought in the summary of different theories, identification of basic themes, and wide range of suggestions for application. And to those very knowledgeable about research on styles, we offer our reflections and personal experiences.

Our approach is comprehensive, but we do not attempt to cover the entire field. We provide theory to enable informed and wise use of the concepts. We offer practical suggestions and urge readers to decide thoughtfully which applications best suit their situations.

The concept of style is both complex and simple. Each view is partially true, and each can be dangerous alone. An oversimplified view can lead to naive action, yet a complex view can result in no action at all. The message of diversity of style is timely and important, and in this book we invite you to join us in finding ways for schools to give all students the opportunity to fulfill their potential.

The Revision

When we wrote the original version of this book in 1985, we were primarily concerned about the need for educational practitioners to make sense of a burgeoning and fascinating area called *learning styles*. At that time, a number of prominent researchers had shared their thoughts and resources with teachers, but no single source pulled the ideas together.

One of our major concerns was to focus on the concept of learning styles as more than labels and models. The notion that people are distinctly different in ways that they learn and make meaning for themselves is of vital importance to educators. Whether one uses the labels of auditory, visual, kinesthetic, concrete/sequential, or abstract/random matters less than the fact that individual student differences are respected and accommodated.

We were frankly concerned in the early '80s about the competition among learning style researchers and the commercialization associated with applications. Teachers wanted to know what to do about the information because they were quick to accept the validity of style differences. They were genuinely excited to find "research" legitimacy for theories they had recognized for years in their teaching experiences. Yet, when it came to the application, the variety of labels and messages from researchers became an obstacle. Teachers often would tell us they were frustrated with the inherent contradictions they saw in the various models.

Our initial work was geared toward identifying the major concepts and giving teachers generic ways to use the information. We said at that time, and still believe, that educators must know that a variety of approaches and models for learning styles exist. If educators focus on only one model, they tend to want all students to fit into the specific categories and characteristics of that model. A combination and crossover of models is usually the most accurate description of a person's style. In our classes, teachers use several learning style instruments to build a profile of themselves and identify their strongest traits and most consistent characteristics.

Our conclusion, after more than 25 years of working in the field, is to encourage teachers to know that there are several valid models of learning styles, and then concentrate on the major concepts using the specific labels as examples. It is not necessary to know each of the approaches in detail. For example, Gardner's description of eight intelligences might help me understand the strong visual spatial traits of my own learning style, and Jung's description of introversion might "fit," but I don't need to study four other learning models to be able to make valuable applications in my teaching. In reality, researchers find much agreement on the major concepts and issues of learning styles. And they often overlap in labeling the different patterns of learning, though their terms are not exactly congruent.

In addition to knowing strengths, it is very useful for teachers to understand their own and their students' areas of weakness. When a student does not have a strong auditory ability, classes heavily dependent on lectures will be difficult. When a teacher does not have a strong intuitive style, it will be more challenging for him or her to point out connecting relationships and possibilities.

In this new edition of *Marching to Different Drummers,* we intend to help educators focus on learning styles theories by presenting the term with a small "l" and a small "s": learning styles instead of Learning Styles. It is important to focus on the practical accommodation of individual differences through a variety of learning style models. By the same token, we very much value the extensive research that has given credence and depth to this area.

Thus, this book describes the major learning style models. It also addresses a variety of applications of style knowledge, arguing that they are related. For example, it is contradictory for an administrator to encourage teachers to accommodate students' learning styles and then to evaluate all teachers with a single approach. It also is contradictory to encourage teaching that values diversity and then to establish a rigid, standardized curriculum. We addressed a number of these issues in the original book and expand on them here.

Throughout the original edition, we talked about learning styles as an "approach," not a program. In this book, we continue to disavow the idea of a "program." We are committed to honoring individual differences, differences that must be respected if a person is going to be a successful learner, teacher, or administrator. We cannot talk about individual differences and then promote a single program—even a single learning style program—for everyone.

Finally, this revision addresses the importance of knowledge about students' culture and recent discoveries about the functioning of the brain. Both of these areas contribute to understanding and respecting an individual's unique ways of learning.

Our Perspectives and Personal Biases

We have studied and observed style in a number of different situations. We know about style from our experiences as teachers and administrators. We balance that experience with academic research on style. And perhaps most important, we continue to learn about style by sharing the concepts with administrators, teachers, and parents. Working with thousands of thoughtful and talented educators has strengthened our resolve about the importance of style and deepened our understanding of the concepts. These practical experiences and academic reflection provide us with certain perspectives about the theories. And, of course, because our individual styles are reflected in this book, it is pertinent to share some of our biases.

1. Individual human differences are positive and should be a resource to schools. We agree with Tomlinson, who wrote that "effective schooling should expand the differences between students rather than restrict them" (in Mackenzie, 1983, p. 13). When students learn and grow in their own ways, differences are pronounced. When we decide we want to value differences, we make decisions that expand diversity rather than seek conformity and inappropriate uniformity.

2. Active recognition of individual differences challenges any "best" answer for an educational question. We have to ask, Best for whom, in what situation, and under what circumstances? In their description of the school improvement processes, Joyce, Hersh, and McKibbin make clear early on that

> there simply is no best model for a school. . . . There are many effective models for schooling, but they do not work equally well for all children, nor do they achieve all purposes to the same degree. (1983, p. 9)

Nor can any one program or instructional strategy be "best" for every student.

3. Differences in style are more than variations in behavior. When I act differently from you, it is because my behavior makes sense to me. Behavior "makes sense" because it is an external reflection of how I understand a situation. Thus, the study of style must both explore differences in behavior and recognize the roots of the behavior. Following this reasoning, fundamental characteristics of style will be reflected in various aspects of behavior: in learning, teaching, administration, and personality in general. These areas must be studied together, or we run the risk of shallow applications. For example, we would want to avoid "doing" learning styles for students while treating all the staff the same.

4. *The variety of perspectives on style and diverse models proposed by researchers offer a rich source of theories, experiences, and suggestions for educational applications.* We should draw from various theories to the extent that they can aid our particular situations. In this book we do not advocate a single model but urge readers to study thoughtfully, examine the perspective and bias of the researchers, form a personal approach to style, and select appropriate ideas for application. Part III of this book offers ideas on how to proceed with this process.

5. *We believe in the importance of the individual teacher's decisions in the classroom.* In his review of effective school research, Mackenzie (1983) says, "No strategy works in isolation from the teacher's judgment and discrimination" (p. 10). Thus, knowledge of styles should provide guidance for wise judgments. This book is designed as a sourcebook for the hundreds of decisions educators face each day.

6. *We are enthusiastic about the power provided by knowledge of styles, but we also recognize this knowledge is not a panacea for problems in schools.* Knowing about differences in style will not make good educators out of cynical, incompetent teachers or administrators. Knowledge of styles will not guarantee effectiveness or excellence in schools. But it does point us in the direction of using the unique talents of both adults and children to make our schools better for all.

User's Guide

This book has three parts. In the first section, we discuss diversity in education and argue for more accommodation of differences. We define style, provide some background into style research, and address the impact of culture and the knowledge of the brain's functioning. In part two, we describe applications of style in seven areas. In the final section, we identify common questions and issues, and discuss applications, implementation, and staff development. For further study, we provide a comprehensive annotated bibliography.

We look at seven major research models and provide an example of application for each. The seven we chose to feature represent major efforts historically and conceptually. Carl Jung's work is a comprehensive study of personality and applications that have evolved through nearly a century of examination. Herman A. Witkin's work is the catalyst for the most extensive and in-depth research on cognitive style conducted in the past 50 years. The modality information, represented here by Walter Barbe and Raymond Swassing and by Rita and Kenneth Dunn, has consistently intrigued educators. The work of the Dunns, Anthony Gregorc, and Bernice McCarthy has brought these concepts directly to teachers. This new addition includes a chapter addressing Howard Gardner's theory of multiple intelligences.[1] As in the first edition, we only touch upon the work of these researchers. We urge readers to study the original sources listed in the annotated bibliography for a fuller understanding of each model.

We invite and encourage you to approach the book with your own style: browse, skip around, read, and reflect. We have also attempted to address the different ways you can know about style by including personal examples, research findings, practical applications, and philosophical implications. We hope that as you read you will discover new understandings about style and raise new questions about the topic.

Some of the book is factual (it reports information), and some is interpretive (it synthesizes our experiences and beliefs). Many of the ideas will provoke questions. The more one studies individual differences, the more complexities one finds. This fact alone reinforces our belief in the importance of the concepts and the need for further exploration.

---

[1] While Gardner makes a distinction between his theory of intelligences and learning styles, there is enough substantial overlap in the concepts to argue that it belongs in this book. Indeed, each of the learning style and cognitive style models described has its own unique and idiosyncratic definitions. Bringing them together is a major purpose of this book.

Some ideas are so simple that experienced educators will recognize them immediately. But acting on concepts is never simple; practicing personalized education is a challenge for even the most experienced among us. We need both the inspiration of theory and the wisdom of experience to guide us.

And so, as always, teachers and administrators are called upon to bring to bear the talents and skills that make them good at their jobs, especially the ability to keep their "heads in the clouds" while their "feet are planted firmly on the ground" (Guild, 1982, p. 6).

Part I

Diversity in Education

1

Diversity and Learning

*Without an **understanding*** of the unique meanings
existing for the individual, the problems of helping
him effectively are almost insurmountable.

—ARTHUR COMBS

We have never met an educator who believed all learners were the
same. Yet visits to schools throughout the world might convince us
otherwise. Too often, educators continue to emphasize uniformity
while paying lip service to the principle of diversity.

We have consciously chosen to open this book with a discussion
of diversity and learning. In a book about individual differences in
learning, we would be remiss not to talk directly about the educational implications of diversity. We believe that any discussion of
diversity should recognize the importance of style differences. It is
this perspective that we address here.

Uniformity and School Practices

Educators know that students learn in different ways; the experience of teaching confirms this every day. In addition, well-accepted
theories and extensive research illustrate and document learning differences. Most educators can talk about learning differences, whether
by the name of learning styles, cognitive styles, psychological type,
or multiple intelligences.

We also know that an individual learner's culture, family background, and socioeconomic level affect his or her learning. The context in which someone grows and develops has an important impact on learning. Learners also bring their own individual talents and interests to the learning situation.

Still, uniformity continues to dominate school practices. More than 50 years ago, Nathaniel Cantor observed that "the public elementary and high schools and colleges generally project what they consider to be the proper way of learning which is uniform for all students" (1946/1972, p. 102). In 50 years, too little has changed. Most schools illustrate the sameness of curriculum content, instructional methods, and evaluation practices. We see students using the same textbooks and the same materials for learning. They work at the same pace on the same quantity of material. They study the same content and work through the same curriculum on the same schedule. Teachers talk with whole groups of students, delivering the same information at the same time to everyone. And, of course, schools use the same tests for all to measure the success of the learning.

Is this kind of sameness always wrong? Surely, given the task of educating large numbers of people, efficiency justifies some consistency and uniformity in the process. Even more valid is the argument for general standards and equality across schools, districts, and states. This is a realistic perspective, but to better match beliefs about diversity with practice, we must address the imbalance between uniformity and diversity.

At present, schools are heavily biased toward uniformity over diversity. An appropriate balance must be determined thoughtfully with attention to beliefs, theories, and research rather than efficiency. We need to decide intentionally what should be uniform and what should be diverse and strive toward putting into practice what we say we believe.

In one sense, the current imbalance is easily understood. Sameness is always easier to accommodate than difference, and education practices often have been developed to consciously promote the same education for all students. We have few teaching models that honor both consistent values and diversity.

A clarification is needed here. Attention to diversity does not mean "anything goes." Honoring diversity does not imply a lack of clear beliefs and strong values. There are some absolutes in education. For example, every learner can benefit from an outstanding teacher and an engaging learning experience. The challenge is to identify what should be the same in schools and what should be different. It's important to decide

- What outcomes should be expected for all students?
- What experiences should every student have?
- What curriculum should be uniform?
- How can educators work toward a common mission while honoring diversity?

These questions do not have simple answers, but we must explore them to accommodate individual differences in the classroom.

Attending to Diversity

There is an urgent need to address the balance between uniformity and diversity because the current imbalance is seriously damaging many learners, teachers, and curriculums. A limited acknowledgment of individual learning differences encourages a continual search for the one "best" way for students to learn, teachers to teach, and the curriculum to be studied. There is ample proof over the years—in reading, mathematics, writing, and foreign language instruction, for example—that it is futile to search for the single best way to achieve a broad educational outcome, in large part because learners do not fit a single mold.

Students who do not learn through whatever the current "best approach" happens to be are too often labeled "disabled" because their way of learning does not respond to that particular method. To further complicate the situation, the method becomes the identified deficit and the target for remediation. For example, in reading, remediation in phonics, which is a strategy, often becomes the target for learning. In a typical situation, a young learner who initially was not successful learning to read with a phonic approach receives additional instruction in phonics. The overarching goal, in this case the ability to read, is lost as the school emphasizes the specific practice of the deficit technique. Remediating a deficit rather than teaching the desired skill through the student's strength is the norm in too many schools.

The same pattern is evident in behavioral areas where, for example, an active, hands-on learner who does not have the opportunity to use that approach in a positive way in the classroom is described as lacking self-control and labeled disruptive or hyperactive. It disturbs many educators to see the tremendous increase in the number of students medicated for attention deficit disorder (ADD) and attention deficit hyperactivity disorder (ADHD) without an examination of their learning styles. Thomas Armstrong, a former special education teacher and a proponent of the multiple intelligences theories, addressed this issue.

> The traits that are associated with ADD—hyperactivity, distractibility, and impulsivity—can result from a number of causes. For example, a child may be hyperactive or inattentive because of being bored with a lesson, anxious about a bully, upset about a divorce, allergic to milk, temperamental by nature, or a hundred other things. Research suggests, though, that once adults have labeled and medicated the child—and the medication works—these more complex questions are all too often forgotten. By rushing to drugs and labels, we may be leaving more difficult problems to fester under the surface. (1995, p. 42)

The emphasis on uniformity is also a serious disadvantage for students whose culture has taught them behaviors and beliefs that are different from the majority norm. Students whose families value collaboration are told to be independent. Students whose culture values spontaneity are told to exercise self-control. Students who are rewarded in their families for being social are told to work quietly and alone. Hale-Benson (1986) points out: "A duality of socialization is required of Black people. Black children have to be prepared to imitate the 'hip,' 'cool,' behavior of the culture in which they live and at the same time to take on those behaviors that are necessary to be upwardly mobile" (p. 62). This cultural clash often causes students to struggle in school, and yet their individual strengths, if valued, respected, and promoted, might bring them success and increase their self-confidence.

Teachers, too, suffer from the imbalance between uniformity and diversity, especially when they are evaluated with uniform processes. Numerous educators—including John Goodlad, Roland Barth, and Ted Sizer—have written eloquently about the value of diversity of teaching styles. We do not have evidence of one best way to teach, just as we don't know of one best way to learn.

An emphasis on uniformity creates competition rather than collaboration among teachers. While identification of specific teaching *skills* can be uniform, diversity of teaching *styles* can and should be a school's strength. For example, all teachers can be held accountable for thoughtful planning, but that planning could be linear and sequential for one teacher and holistic and conceptual for another. The plan books of these teachers would look very different, and they should be evaluated differently, too.

Distinct approaches to content instruction, curriculum, classroom organization, and special education programming come and go over the years. It is unrealistic to expect that a particular approach will be successful for all learners. This expectation only leads to disappointment and another swing of the education pendulum. After the pendulum swings to the other extreme, and that approach also fails with many learners, the pendulum swings yet again. One example is foreign language instruction, where an emphasis on spoken language trades off with a structured grammatical approach. Instead of an either-or mentality, many experienced teachers know that using the best of both approaches benefits many learners.

Accommodating Diversity

To create a more realistic balance between uniformity and diversity, we must address four issues.

1. Understanding Differences

The first issue is to develop a deep understanding of individual differences in learning. The research and theories on cognitive style and learning style adequately document the learning differences among individuals. While these theories are familiar to many educators, and generally accepted, their application is relatively shallow.

For example, many teachers know that it is important to provide a "visual" learner with visual information. But if the visual is words on an overhead projector mimicking the words spoken orally, this is a superficial accommodation of the learner's style. Far more significant would be an image, symbol, or visual representation of the information so that the visual learner could learn through his or her strengths.

Many teachers know that the kinesthetic learner needs hands-on experiences. A deeper understanding of these learners tells us that the experiences should come early in the process while the initial understanding of the concepts and skills are being developed, not just during practice time. Yet many times these learners are asked to "understand" first, then "do" later. The kinesthetic learner needs to manipulate the science equipment to understand the concepts, and she will learn abstract math concepts while doing the measurement project or even after it's completed. The kinesthetic learners' impatience to get started sometimes causes teachers to demand that they explain what they will do before they start. This is difficult for these students, since the doing leads to the understanding and the explaining.

Learning styles research and resources are rich with examples to help develop appropriate activities for different learners. But if the activities are not guided by a consistent and deep understanding of the significance of learning differences, the activities will be a cursory attempt to implement these concepts. Learning styles labels are simply a tool; the diverse behaviors we see in the classroom are reflections of much deeper cognitive processes.

Not all learners who share a certain label are alike. A "visual" learner who is also "concrete sequential" seeks visual order and would benefit from a linear diagram of material. A "visual" learner who is also "abstract random" responds to design and would be drawn to a mind-map format for organizing information. A careful study of the major concepts of learning styles is necessary for the practical application of this theory in schools.

2. Equity and Equality

The second major issue is a need to understand the difference between equity and equality. We often justify uniformity in education with the theory that the goal of schooling is to offer equal learning experiences for all students. We value equality and applaud examples as a confirmation of fairness to all. Yet, equal experiences do not provide equality for diverse learners. The word equity is far more significant and appropriate in this case.

Equity means "fair" and "just," implying equal opportunity, which often means unequal action. Felix Frankfurter wrote, "It is a wise man who said that there is no greater inequality than the equal treatment of unequals" (1949, p. 184). David Elkind echoes that same sentiment in his book *The Hurried Child:* "Recognizing special needs is not discriminatory; on the contrary, it is the only way that true equality can be attained" (Elkind, 1981, p. 22).

Administrators and school boards grapple with the equity issue each time they address the "fairness" of standard class sizes, when some schools and some classes have more children who need special attention from the teacher. Should schools with large immigrant populations, and the concurrent special language instruction requirements, be staffed with the same formula as a school with a homogeneous English-speaking student body? Should students at both of these schools be required to take the same curriculum and the same tests? What is "fair"? What is "equitable"?

In the classroom, teachers regularly confront issues of equity with assignments and quizzes. Is it "fair" to adapt an assignment, expecting some students to produce more in quantity, such as longer essays, or in quality, such as completing harder geometry proofs? Many schools and teachers think so, and they regularly diversify expectations for students.

3. Ends Versus Means

The third important issue addresses the distinction between the ends and the means. It is possible to strive for uniform outcomes but to intentionally diversify the means for achieving them. Schools can identify basic skill and knowledge goals for all students, yet these uniform expectations do not automatically dictate a uniform approach, nor a uniform curriculum, for reaching the goals. In an extensive argument *for* national and state standards, Paul Gagnon (1995) states:

What is a subject-matter essential, or "standard," and what is not? It is specific, not abstract, but it does not descend to detail. . . . [T]he word "framework," too, means what it says; it leaves the third step—course design and pedagogy—to the school and the teacher. They must have the authority to make the choices most important to them and to their students: the topics and questions by which to teach the essentials, the day-to-day content of instruction, the materials and methods best suited to their students and to their own strengths. (p. 72)

One familiar controversy is in the field of early reading. For years, educators have debated phonetic versus meaning-based approaches. The research presented articulately and convincingly by proponents of both approaches usually cites a successful achievement statistic of 65 to 70 percent. If we accept that students learn in different ways, it should be evident that different approaches to reading work for different students.

Therefore, is it possible that a majority of students can learn to read with a phonetic approach and also a majority of students can learn to read with a meaning-based approach? Probably yes, especially with good instruction. There is undoubtedly an overlap of 35 to 40 percent of students who learn with either approach and who appear as successful statistics in both studies. However, if you view this research by looking at those who are not successful, the 30 percent minority, you see students who need attention. These students are probably not as flexible in their ways of learning and will learn best when their dominant style is accommodated.

Indeed, the cognitive style research on field-dependence-independence supports this conclusion (see Chapter 9). Field-independent learners profit from a part-to-whole approach like phonics while field-dependent learners are more successful with the whole-to-part approach of a meaning-based strategy. Because this cognitive style dimension is bipolar, we would expect 25 to 30 percent of a class to strongly represent each specific learning style pattern, with the remaining 40 percent in the middle. When the learners with a strong, specific learning style approach are forced to learn in a manner opposite their style preference, they must put energy into shifting approaches before they can concentrate on the skill to be mastered. This is similar to trying to learn to write calligraphy with your less preferred hand. Eventually you would gain some skill, but your learning would have been more efficient, enjoyable, and successful if you used your strength—your preferred hand—in the first place.

As another example, it would be typical to find a goal of "global awareness" in the curriculum of a school district; yet individual schools and teachers might accomplish this outcome in very different ways. When specific topics and timelines are required, the opportunity to personalize the curriculum is compromised. Some teachers can bring their own experiences and expertise to teaching geared to this goal and enrich the curriculum immensely. Additionally, students will benefit from a survey type approach to global studies one time, such as a world history course, and an in-depth approach another time, such as the study of the Chinese Revolution. These options, in the "means" of education, honor the differences among students and teachers.

4. Distinguishing Skill and Style

The fourth issue is the importance of distinguishing between skill and style. It is possible for all students to be skilled in basic areas that educators agree upon, for example, that all students would be competent readers, writers, and spellers. The practice of diversity implies that there are a variety of ways to achieve these required skills and individual ways to demonstrate achievement. Uniform competencies and skills can be articulated, but educators can honor stylistic learning differences for achieving and demonstrating those skills.

For example, teachers often debate the value of specific grammatical instruction. How much time should be spent teaching punctuation skills, or are they best learned in context of written work in the classroom? Is it "best" to teach the rules for math computation, and then apply them in practice problems? Or would tackling a problem initially give students a reason for knowing the rules? Most textbooks have answered these questions by consistently building from the part to the whole, the simple to the more complex. But teachers often find that teaching "backward" in the text responds to many students' ways of learning. Many adults exhibit this style of learning when they try skiing a few times before taking lessons or when they "teach" themselves a new program on the computer, then read the manual. Students need similar options.

When we value diversity, we strive to expand our repertoire of instructional strategies, methods of assessment and evaluation, curriculum content and organization, and teaching styles. Decisions are based on the impact for an individual student's success, not the "one right way." Roland Barth (1980) stated it quite clearly:

> Pluralism rather than uniformity, eclecticism rather than ortho-
> doxy, offer our greatest hope for minimizing dissonance and
> maximizing learning. . . . Diversity is abundant and free. Used
> wisely, deliberately, and constructively, it offers an untapped,
> renewable resource available to the public schools. We should
> learn to use it well. (p. 16)

Perhaps most important, honoring diversity gives us an opportunity to practice what we preach. We know people are different from one another, that each individual is unique. Every classroom should exemplify practices as evidence of that knowledge.

2

Style: One Kind of Difference

The wise man shows his wisdom in separation,
in graduation, and his scale of creatures and of
merits is as wide as nature. The foolish have no
range in their scale, but suppose every man is as
every other man.

—Ralph Waldo Emerson

Some people have a distinct style of dress. Others have a style of speech that reflects their regional roots. Some athletes bring their own style to a sport.

When we use "style" in these ways, we are noting recognizable patterns. "Outsiders" see this pattern, associate it with the person, and find it typical and relatively consistent. Although people do not always dress and speak in the same way, their usual behavior can be predictable enough.

The way we perceive the world governs how we think, make judgments, and form values about experiences and people. This unique aspect of our humanness is what we call "style." It is based on the fact that, as Carl Jung (1921/1971) observed, "Besides the many individual differences in human psychology there are also typical differences" (p. 3).

How about you? Do you notice immediately when a friend or colleague gets a new pair of glasses or changes hairstyles? Have you ever described a car accident only to discover that another witness reported it quite differently? Do you try to figure out what an abstract painting portrays, or do you react to its colors and the mood it engenders? Differences in perception help explain why people see things differently even when they look at the same scene.

Consider your morning routine. Do you have a daily pattern for dressing, showering, and eating breakfast? Does it bother you when this pattern is disturbed? Or would having a rigid routine bore you? Your daily behavior patterns often reflect your thinking processes. Those of us who order our mornings in a systematic, linear way probably form our ideas and think that way, too.

Are you intrigued by the challenge of puzzles, or do you think they're a waste of time? Do you know how many countries are on the continent of Africa? Do you want to know the practical purpose of a task before you are willing to give it a try? Do you buy a new car by carefully weighing data from automotive reports, or do you simply buy the model and color you've always wanted? When you disagree with someone, do you worry how he or she will take your comments? Just as differences in what motivates and interests each of us reflect our unique perspectives, so do a person's criteria for decisions and judgments reflect his or her style.

These basic and consistent patterns in personality influence many aspects of personal and professional behavior. In general, they can be called personality styles. When they affect learning, we call them learning styles. Patterns reflected in teaching are called teaching styles. Management patterns are called leadership or administrative styles.

Assumptions About Style

When introduced to the concept of style, people often say, "You mean there are other people like me?" It's a comment said half in jest, but often with a serious note. "I really am OK!" usually follows, and they have lots of questions. Some typical comments and questions have led us to identify a few general assumptions about style, which we will explore further throughout this book.

- **"Yes, Virginia, everyone has style." Each person is complex, and yet each person is predictable, too.** It's the predictable side of people that announces their style. These patterns give us familiar ways to approach life and provide us with stability, maturity, and psychological health. They also allow those with whom we associate to interact with us in a reliable manner. They give us some things in common with other people, but their particular combination and intensity make each of us unique. As you study words that describe style, it will be helpful to think about your own style profile.

• **"I'm OK, you're OK." Style is basically neutral.** While I may find someone's pattern of speech "strange," I understand that it is natural for that person and probably for his or her family, friends, and neighbors. Some people do have speech disabilities, but a style of speech indicates a difference, not necessarily a problem.

• **"Still waters run deep." Style is basically stable, but behaviors emanating from style traits may change according to the situation.** If I'm an exacting, detail-oriented perfectionist, this trait probably has been with me from childhood and will remain with me throughout life. But the behaviors that reflect this trait will most likely adapt to each situation. I may carefully organize my files at the office, but at home I'm resigned to a more flexible organization of the refrigerator, which the whole family uses. I might be generally attentive to social cues, but my intense focus when I'm working on a big project might preclude such niceties as saying a simple "good morning" to my coworkers.

• **"Yes, but . . ." Style is not absolute.** Just as a staunch Republican may vote for a certain Democratic candidate, so too there will be specific exceptions to pervasive style patterns. I may typically make decisions in an objective, cool-headed way—except when they relate to money. However, if my behavior regularly fluctuates in a certain aspect of my life, it is possible that either I don't have a defined pattern for that task or contrasting patterns pull me in different directions.

• **"I could if I wanted to." Style alone does not determine competence.** I may not balance my checkbook, but I am able to do it if I decide it's necessary or my job requires it. I may not notice your new hairstyle, but if you point it out, I'm certainly capable of seeing it. At some point, preferred style does affect certain tasks by making them easier or harder. Thus, style can be related to a person's strengths and weaknesses. But style does not automatically indicate competence.

- **"It takes one to know one." Style traits are easier to recognize in others if we personally understand those characteristics.** People who know a Maine accent, for example, immediately recognize that speech pattern. If I hear a practical question, I tune in if I, too, value practicality. If I don't understand someone, it's likely that our styles are very different, and it becomes more difficult to achieve that understanding.

These assumptions and examples help us to see both the simple and complex nature of style. While many things are known about style, we also have much to discover and explain. As you read further, expect to encounter complex issues about style theories. These theories help us understand basic human nature, but they also require careful consideration to take root in our consciousness and find their way to daily application.

Style and Education

Education is a people business. Perhaps every issue, decision, and problem that we deal with in schools is basically a human relations situation. The effectiveness of curriculum, instruction, discipline, management, and community relations as well as the degree of academic achievement often can be traced to the ability of people to identify common purposes and work productively together. We find quality and excellence in learning and teaching where there is open communication, high expectations, positive climate and morale, commitment of community and parents, and talented, caring professionals.

Because we know that people are different, education is a business about diversity. It is about the different goals people have for education. It is about the different programs people want in schools. It is about various ways adults exhibit their competencies in their work. And it is about the multitude of ways students learn.

Yet simply accepting the existence of diversity is not the same as putting that acceptance into practice. We make rules for a school assuming that everyone values and interprets them in the same way.

We talk with staff members and students and assume that our intentions are communicated as uniformly as our words and sentences are structured. We search for the "right" or "best" programs and methods for helping students to learn, as if they all learn in the same way.

Here's where the study of style is particularly important. Knowing that people see different things helps us communicate with more depth. Knowing that people have different beliefs and values helps us understand the various interests and needs of a diverse school population. Recognizing the importance of style helps us create the atmosphere and experiences that encourage each individual—adult and child—to reach his or her full potential.

3

Culture and Style

That need for a sense of individuality is in every
human being and one must not ignore it.

—Eleanor Roosevelt

When you describe a culture, do you include ethnicity, religion, gender, and socioeconomic background? What words do you use to describe characteristics of your own culture? When do such descriptions feel comfortable, and when do they become simplistic stereotypes? Are you "typical" of your culture in some ways, and are you unique in other ways?

As you think about these questions for yourself and discuss them with people of various cultures, it's likely that the responses will be complex. Thus, it's no surprise that when we ask how culture affects learning, we broach a sensitive area.

We know that culture and learning are connected in important ways. Early life experiences and the values of a person's culture affect both the expectations and the processes of learning. If this relationship is true, could we then assume that students who share cultural characteristics have common learning style patterns? Does culture create a learning style, and how would we know this? These questions are both important and controversial.

They are important because we need all the information we can get to help every learner succeed in school, and because a deep understanding of the learning process should provide a framework for curriculum and instructional decisions. They also are important questions because success for the diverse populations in schools calls for continual reexamination of educators' assumptions, expectations, and biases. And finally, they are important considerations because every decision in education must be examined for its impact on an individual student's learning.

Such questions are controversial because information about a group of people often leads to naive inferences about individual members of that group. Additionally, in the search for explanations of the continued achievement difference between students of color and mainstream white students, there is an understandable sensitivity about causes and effects. It is all too easy to confuse descriptions of differences with explanations for deficits. The questions also are controversial because they force us to confront philosophical issues in the uniformity versus diversity debate. Is equality of instruction synonymous with equity of educational opportunity for all? Is the purpose of schooling to create a "melting pot" or "a salad bowl"?

A highly public example of how sensitive these issues are occurred in 1987 when New York state published a booklet for educators aimed at decreasing the student dropout rate. A small section of the booklet described learning styles typical of minority students and identified certain patterns associated with African American students. These descriptions became the subject of intense scrutiny and animated debate. The descriptions were eventually removed from the booklet, but a review panel concluded that "learning style and behavioral tendency do exist, and [that] students from particular socialization and cultural experiences often possess approaches to knowledge which are highly functional in the indigenous home environment and can be capitalized upon to facilitate performance in academic settings" (New York State Regent's Report ms. in Claxton, 1990, p. 6).

A deep understanding of both culture and learning style is important for all educators, though the subject must be addressed carefully. The relationship of the values of the culture in which a child is currently living, or from which a child has roots, and the learning expectations and experiences in the classroom is directly related to the child's school success academically, socially, and emotionally.

The Nature vs. Nurture Issue

If a classroom teacher is to facilitate successful learning opportunities for all learners, he or she must "know" the learner. This includes knowing about innate personality traits we call "style" and also learned cultural values that affect behavior. The learner, of any age, is a product of nature and nurture. We each are born with predispositions for learning in certain ways. We also are products of external influences, especially within our immediate family, extended community, and culture.

Researchers confirm that learning patterns are a function of both nature and nurture. Myers (1990) asserts: "Type development starts at a very early age. The hypothesis is that type is inborn, an innate predisposition like right- or left-handedness, but the successful development of type can be greatly helped or hindered by environment from the beginning" (p. 176). Many researchers describe the importance of socialization within the family, immediate culture, and wider culture. They agree with Ramirez (1989) that "cultural differences in children's learning styles develop through their early experience" (p. 4). Gardner (1991) echoes this perspective: "[W]e are as much creatures of our culture as we are creatures of our brain" (p. 38).

Sometimes people wonder which is more important: innate personality traits or the influence of culture? This question has no clear answer. The most accurate response is probably "it depends." Variables such as the congruence of innate traits with cultural influences; the support, or lack of it, within the environment for preferred behaviors and for taking risks; and general life successes will influence how learning style is shaped. When my culture supports my individuality, I grow and develop in healthy ways. When my family encourages my uniqueness, I learn to trust my own innate predisposition. If, however, I do not innately fit the expectations of a "typical girl" or "typical African American," I become aware of the lack of congruence of my inner self with external expectations, and I have to reconcile those differences. Sometimes that reconciliation gives me more strengths and a wider range of behaviors. At other times, it leads to conflict and uncertainties. Both results confirm the important roles of nature and nurture in shaping a person's approach to life—and to learning.

Every child of every culture, race, ethnicity, socioeconomic status, gender, age, ability, and talent deserves to have an equal opportunity to be successful in school. Knowing each student's culture is essential for providing successful learning opportunities. Understanding learning differences will help educators facilitate, structure, and validate successful learning for every student.

Reports About Culture and Learning Style

Reports about culture and learning style consistently agree that within a group, variations among individuals are as great as commonalties. Even as we acknowledge that culture affects learning styles, we know that distinct learning style patterns don't fit a specific cultural group. "Researchers have clearly established that there is no single or dual learning style for the members of any cultural, national, racial, or religious group" (Dunn, 1997, pp. 74–75).

This important point is often verbally acknowledged, but ignored in practice. Cox and Ramirez (1981) explain the result:

> Recognition and identification of these average differences have had both positive and negative effects in education. The positive effect has been the development of an awareness of the types of learning that our public schools tend to foster . . . . The negative effect[,] . . . arising primarily from common problems associated with looking at mean differences[,] is [that] the great diversity within a culture is ignored and a construct which should be used as a tool for individualization becomes yet another label for categorizing and evaluating. (p. 61)

Many reports contend that African Americans or Hispanic Americans or girls learn in certain common ways. Where is this information coming from? In general, there are three sources of information about learning styles and culture.

Descriptions and Profiles

The first source includes descriptions and profiles of learners of certain cultural groups written by people familiar with these groups to sensitize those outside the culture to children's experiences within the culture. Descriptions of minority students' learning patterns often are contrasted with the "majority" white Anglo students' ways of learning and with expectations in the schools designed by this majority group.

There are a variety of descriptions of typical learning patterns of African Americans (Hale-Benson, 1986; Shade, 1989; Hilliard, 1989); descriptions of Mexican Americans (Ramirez, 1989; Vasquez, 1991; Berry, 1979; Cox & Ramirez, 1981); descriptions of Native Americans (Bert & Bert, 1992; Moore, 1990; Shade, 1989); and descriptions of Asian Americans (Moore, 1990). Gilligan's (1993) work on gender has been used to describe girls' ways of learning.

Reports note that family and personal relationships are important to Mexican Americans, and these learners are comfortable with cognitive generalities and patterns (Cox & Ramirez, Vasquez). These traits explain why Mexican American students often seek a personal relationship with a teacher and are more comfortable with broad concepts rather than distinct facts and specifics. Observations of African American students' learning styles report their comfort with oral experiences, physical activity, and strong personal relationships (Shade, Hilliard). These call for classroom work that includes collaboration, discussion, and active projects. Observational descriptions indicate that Native Americans generally develop acute visual discrimination and skills in the use of imagery, perceive globally, and have reflective thinking patterns (Shade, Moore, Bert & Bert). Thus, schooling should emphasize visual information, provide quiet "think time," and establish a context for new information. Asian Americans are described as serious, independent, content oriented, and focused (Moore). This description implies that working alone, especially on serious content, is appealing to these learners. Girls are said to value relationships, be verbal, and be social. In the classroom they like working in groups and having opportunities to share (Gilligan).

The same authors report that mainstream white male Americans value independence, analytic thinking, objectivity, and accuracy. These values translate into learning experiences that focus on information, competition, tests, grades, and critical thinking. It is no surprise that these patterns are prevalent in most schools because they were established and are generally administered by mainstream white males. The further away from this style of education a student is, the more difficulty he or she has adjusting.

Research Study Descriptions

Another way we know about the links between culture and learning style is research study descriptions of specific groups. In this class of inquiry, researchers administer learning/cognitive style assessments to produce a profile of a particular cultural group, to make comparisons with previously studied groups (usually mainstream white Americans), or to validate a particular instrument for cross-cultural application. While a variety of published studies use this approach, it is important to realize that they are based on various assessment instruments that "measure" learning styles in different ways. (Style instruments are discussed in more detail in Chapter 15.)

Many of these instruments are self-report. In other words, the adult or student fills out a response to a series of questions, and the frequency of responses indicates certain preferences for specific approaches to learning. When a person is asked to respond to specific words and questions, the language is interpreted through personal (cultural) experience. Some assessment instruments test a person's strengths, or the ability to do tasks with a certain approach. When strengths are tested and learning style inferred from the results of these instruments, a great deal of variety exists within like-cultural groups.

Thus, the information obtained from formal assessments of learning styles of specific cultural groups has been based on different ways of assessing and describing style. Yet results of different studies are often compared, ignoring or diminishing the relevance of the type of assessment instrument in the report of the findings. The variation in type of assessment instrument used often accounts for the seemingly contradictory information reported about groups of learners.

Direct Discussion

The third way we know about learning style and culture is through direct discussion. A number of authors have written about the importance of understanding culture to more effectively facilitate the learning of all students. Cognitive style research, Ramirez (1989) believes, could help contribute to multiethnic education as "a framework to look at and be responsive to diversity within and between cultures" (p. 4).

Shade (1989) comments that: "The examination of a perceptual development from a cultural perspective, however, suggests that perceptual development differs within various ethnocultural groups. It is an erroneous assumption in the teaching-learning process to assume children 'see' the same event, idea, or object in the same way" (p. 151).

From all three sources of "research" we see that culture and learning style are connected, but it is necessary to caution educators about specific application of this information.

Issues and Questions

When educators apply knowledge of culture and learning style to the classroom they face a number of unresolved areas and differences of opinion. Some educators call for explicit knowledge of specific groups' cultural values so that practitioners will be more sensitive and effective with students of that culture. This information is even mandated in certain states as part of their multicultural goals, although, ironically, learning styles information usually is missing. Other educators argue that these descriptions will result in more stereotyping and ultimately in a differentiated, segregated approach to curriculum.

Cox and Ramirez (1981) observe:

> The concept of cognitive or learning styles of minority and other students is one easily over-simplified, misunderstood, or misinterpreted. Unfortunately, it has been used to stereotype minority students or to further label them rather than to identify individual differences that are educationally meaningful. (p. 61)

Ask yourself how much you would want a teacher and a school to know about your own child. Should there be full information in a student's file that is shared with everyone who works with the student? Even when such information exists, some teachers intentionally don't read students' files. They argue that they want to form their own impressions of each learner. Other educators feel that comprehensive background and educational history of each student is invaluable for helping the learner be successful. Why waste time reinventing the wheel? When these same issues are applied to knowledge relating to a specific cultural group, there is also lack of agreement. "The greatest care must be taken to use the concepts as tools for growth and individualization and to avoid their use as labels or stereotypes" (Ramirez, 1989, p. 5).

The relationship of culture and learning style is also addressed in reference to student achievement. Most researchers believe that learning styles are neutral. All learning styles can be successful, but they also could become a stumbling block when overused or applied inappropriately. This concept explains the success or failure of different learning approaches with different tasks, especially as they relate to expectations in schools. There is evidence that students with specific learning style patterns (kinesthetic, field-dependent, sensing, extraversion) underachieve in school. Regardless of their cultural background, students who have these dominant learning style patterns have limited opportunities to use their style strengths in the classroom.

While relating culture, style, and achievement requires much more examination (Guild, McKinney, & Fouts, 1990; Myers, 1974/ 1980), serious inequity results if schools undervalue behaviors that certain cultures foster. Gardner (1991) advises that cultural practices yield "[c]hildren and adults who are characteristic of their own culture and who may appear dysfunctional in a culture that embraces a divergent or opposing set of assumptions" (p. 53). This appearance of dysfunction affects the student's potential for successful achievement. Some students are caught in a no-win situation, unable to be true to their culture or meet school expectations. Irvine and York (1995) are blunt: "The cultures of students of color or their 'way of life' are often incongruous with the expected middle-class cultural values, beliefs, and norms of schools. These cultural differences are major contributions to the school failure of students of color" (p. 489).

Teachers' Cultures

Another unresolved issue is how teachers working from their own cultures and teaching styles can successfully reach the diverse populations in most schools today. What training do teachers need for this challenge? Bennett (1986) is not the only one who believes that "to the extent that teachers teach as they have been taught to learn, and to the extent that culture shapes learning style, students who share a teacher's ethnic background will be favored in class" (p. 96). Bennett also warns that ignoring the effects of culture and learning style affects all students:

> If classroom expectations are limited by our own cultural orientations, we impede successful learners guided by another cultural orientation. If we only teach according to the ways we ourselves learn best, we are also likely to thwart successful learners who may share our cultural background but whose learning styles deviate from our own. (p. 116)

Some argue that teachers play a special role in representing their own culture. "It is incumbent upon Black professionals to identify the intelligences found especially in Black children and to support the pursuit of their strengths" (Hale-Benson, 1986, p. xiii). However, we all have learned successfully from teachers who differed from us in learning style or culture. Often, these were masterful, caring teachers. Sometimes our own motivation helped us learn in spite of the teacher. Yet teachers of all cultural backgrounds and style will have to work conscientiously to provide equity for students as classrooms increasingly reflect the diversity of our society.

It is also important to be willing to confront the issue of cultural identity and self-esteem. Many large city school systems struggle with the appropriateness of ethnically identified schools such as an African American academy. Bilingual programs continue to debate the priority of instruction in students' first languages. All-girl schools, math classes, and science classes are promoted for their affirmative action approach.

The goal of encouraging positive self-esteem would lead one to argue for like-groups at certain stages of development. An acceptance of learning styles demands an approach that develops skills through strengths. Should the same not be said of cultural identity?

Implications

Knowledge of learning styles and of the child's culture helps teachers examine their own instructional practices and become sensitive to providing diverse learning experiences. Intentional instructional diversity will benefit all students. In other words, improved instructional methodologies and practices for certain students will result in improved instruction for all.

A teacher who brings outstanding skills and competencies to his work offers students from all cultures and with varying learning styles greater opportunities for success. The teachers who are successful with students of various cultures want to know all they can about their students so that the learning opportunities and structures they provide are responsive to students' needs. These teachers know that to provide effective instruction, they must accommodate both the cultural values and individual learning styles of their students. Therefore, they are continually interested in learning about their students.

A teacher who cares about and develops methodologies sensitive to the needs of the learners she works with will foster success. Too often, the accommodation of differences is limited to a cultural holiday celebration or a multicultural fair. Even the study of multicultural content often fails to consider the different ways students learn. Thus, serious consideration of culture and learning styles together will offer the opportunity for more depth for culturally sensitive curriculum.

Bennett (1986) emphasizes the value of a learning style perspective:

> The concept of learning styles offers a value-neutral approach for understanding individual differences among ethnically different students. . . . The assumption is that everyone can learn, provided teachers respond appropriately to individual and learning needs. (p. 97)

In a review of learning styles research on culturally diverse students, Irvine and York (1995) echo that sentiment: "[A]ll students are capable of learning, provided the learning environment attends to a variety of learning styles" (p. 494).

While the questions of culture and style are not easy to address, they are crucial to contemplate together. Hilliard (1989) says, "Educators need not avoid addressing the question of style for fear they may be guilty of stereotyping students. Empirical observations are not the same as stereotyping, but the observations must be empirical and must be interpreted properly for each student" (p. 69). Andrew Latham in a 1997 discussion of culture and learning style points out the changing demographics of the school population—70 percent nonwhite or Hispanic by 2026—and the immediate need for teachers to be able to teach a wide variety of students, diverse in their cultures and learning styles.

Explicit, ongoing dialogue about both learning styles and culture will provide educators with valuable information to help more students be successful learners. The goal is equity: true equal opportunity for all learners.

The Brain and Style

Each of us has a gift however seemingly trivial
which is peculiar to him and which, if worthily used,
will be a joy to humanity forever.

—JOHN RUSKIN

Robert Sylwester, a noted expert on the brain and its educational implications, contends that teachers always have been brain researchers. He justifies this belief by citing teachers' experiences observing and facilitating student learning day after day, year after year. This learning, which young children seem to do effortlessly and which continues for life, must be understood in the context of the brain, which is our most complex body organ.

As information about the brain has increased, educators have felt both excited and threatened by the new knowledge. On one hand, it is wonderful to know more clearly how the brain works. On the other hand, it can be baffling, overwhelming, and intimidating when educators consider using brain research in the classroom.

New information about the brain is relevant to many educational theories and applications, and educators operate from a set of assumptions about the brain on a daily basis. We make hundreds of decisions based on our own understanding about how people learn. In this chapter, we focus on the brain's relationship to learning styles.

Basic Connections

The most basic connection is the simple message that every brain is configured differently:

> The marvelous thing about our maturation process is that our individual brains develop very differently. . . . Our brains develop in their own way which lends credence to the idea of multiple intelligences and specializations. (Sylwester in Brandt, 1997, p. 18)

Renate Caine and Geoffrey Caine (1997) have written extensively about the educational implications of knowledge about the brain. They, too, emphasize the singular characteristics of each brain, and one of their brain/mind learning principles is that "every brain is uniquely organized." They explain,

> [W]e all have the same set of systems and yet we are all different. Some of this difference is a consequence of our genetic endowment, some of it is a consequence of differing experiences and differing environments. The differences express themselves in terms of learning styles, differing talents and intelligences, and so on. (p. 108)

The Caines (1997) also say, "[I]n a school or classroom practicing brain-based learning, the importance of different intelligences and learning styles is taken for granted" (p. 20).

When, and if, educators seriously consider the impact of understanding the learning process—by studying the functioning of the brain and understanding individual differences—there could be a revolution in the structure of schooling as we know it. Sylwester argues that this revolution will be initiated by people outside the field of education if educators continue to ignore expanding knowledge about the brain.

Sylwester's book, *A Celebration of Neurons: An Educator's Guide to the Human Brain* (1995), and the Caines' books, *Making Connections: Teaching and the Human Brain* (1991) and *Education on the Edge of Possibility* (1997), are strongly recommended reading. Sylwester does a masterful job of synthesizing a great deal of complex scientific information about the brain for educators. The Caines describe a larger context of education and learning as a natural extension of a knowledge of how people learn.

What We Know About the Brain

In just over 30 years, scientists have been able to study the biology and chemistry of the brain through advanced technology. By being able to watch the electromagnetic fields of blood flow through magnetic resonance imaging (MRI), researchers can look at the direct connections between brain chemistry and social tasks and environment. Dramatic advances in technology have confirmed long-term assumptions about how the brain functions. Additionally, current research techniques have revealed a great deal of new information.

The brain's ability to grow and adapt in response to environmental stimuli is now confirmed. The word "plasticity" describes this ability. Biologically, the brain is composed of a network of neurons that are interconnected in a variety of complex ways. Sylwester describes how brain researcher Gerald Edelman uses the metaphor of a jungle to help people visualize this complex nature of the brain (1995, p. 23). In a jungle, millions of elements overlap and interface with one another in hundreds of complex ways. While each element performs a unique function, the interface among elements creates other functions and dimensions. Many things happen simultaneously, and the layers upon layers of life interact with one another.

The Caines (1991, p. 26) use the metaphor of a city observed from on high. The city is composed of physical structures connected in a variety of ways. Agents within the physical structures make the city work. The physical structures and the agents are clustered in a variety of groups. There are many simultaneous functions operating in parallel while each maintains its uniqueness and distinctiveness.

Both of these metaphors are helpful for understanding the complexity and "messiness" of the brain. We now know clearly that there are many dimensions of interconnectedness within the biology and chemistry of the brain. These different networks cooperate to perform the basic functions of the brain, such as attending, discriminating, selecting, classifying, memorizing, reacting, holding ambiguities, interpreting, and judging. Obviously, most of these functions play an important role in even the simplest learning tasks.

Another vital element in current brain research is the importance of emotions. The brain operates in a social context, and emotions can now be tracked through advanced technology. This has helped us to understand the dominant role emotions play in all aspects of human life. The Caines discuss how the danger of threat in a learning situation causes people to "down shift," thus preventing productive learning from taking place. Both the Caines and Sylwester emphasize the importance of the brain's sensitivity to the social connections in behavior. For the brain to operate at its optimum, it must deal with emotions.

Brain research also addresses the importance of experiences during a child's earliest years. An environment with rich stimuli and a wide variety of experiences does indeed help the brain develop. A young child responds constantly to stimuli, processing his or her own experiences. These actions create new connections and stronger pathways within the physical networks of the brain—connections and pathways that can be relied on later for more challenging and complex learning.

Knowledge about the brain's operations is incomplete. As scientists continue their studies, educators must be alert for new information. In the next generation, we undoubtedly will add a great deal to our knowledge, both about the brain's operations and its implications for education. Some knowledge will confirm much of what teachers have always known, but other information will stretch everyone's professional knowledge.

The Brain and Learning Styles

The study of the brain directly addresses the question of nature and nurture. To what extent is a person born with certain proclivities, talents, and personality, and to what extent does experience shape the individual? This same question is important in learning styles theories.

As we explore brain research, we learn about the uniqueness of each brain from the moment of birth as well as the importance of environmental stimuli. Sylwester (1995) says, "The emotional system emerging from this research is a complex, widely distributed, and error-prone system that defines our basic personality very early in life and is quite resistant to change" (p. 72). Once again, the balance of nature and nurture is confirmed: People are born with unique personalities, but nurture shapes the formation of those personalities.

A second important relationship between brain research and learning styles is the attention focused on a variety of legitimate and valuable ways to learn. Brain researchers report the importance of social context for learning. Learning styles defines social learners as legitimate types of learners, but often this legitimacy is ignored in the classroom. The same is true of active, physical, and kinesthetic learning styles, described in brain research as a learner who explores actively and engages with experiences and problems. This learning approach is considered important for development of a healthy brain, but again, it often is not honored in the classroom. Another example is the learner who easily makes connections and whose mind seems to think in tangents to relate seemingly disparate information. Though brain research confirms the value of this kind of thinking, these global and intuitive learners usually are not appreciated in the classroom.

As we read the descriptions of the brain's function in a learning situation, it is obvious that there are many possible brain pathways that can be activated for successful learning. Further understanding of brain research should make it evident that we need to broaden our perspective of successful learning approaches in the classroom. This will certainly benefit many learning styles that are currently undervalued in school.

A third connection between learning styles and brain research is the direct refinement of messages that the two fields have for each other. For example, Bernice McCarthy studied both learning style differences and the theory of brain hemisphericity when she developed her 4MAT learning style model (see Chapter 12). She defined four distinct learning styles and then described the differences for each brain hemisphere dominance within each learning style. While hemispheric specialization is somewhat more complex than initially assumed when McCarthy began her work, it is still a good example of how brain research helps to refine broader distinctions of learning style characteristics.

By the same token, learning styles can help brain researchers understand more about the unique perceptions of individuals. Brain researchers talk about the brain processing in both wholes and parts. Learning styles theories, particularly in the area of field-dependence and field-independence (described in Chapter 9), can help brain researchers bring more sophistication to that concept. Recently, educators have paid more attention to the importance of emotion to learning. Howard Gardner describes interpersonal and intrapersonal intelligences, both having to do with personal insights and sophisticated applications of emotions. Daniel Goleman's (1995) book *Emotional Intelligence: Why It Can Matter More Than IQ* describes in detail the value of emotions in brain development and the implications for educators.

Finally, brain research and learning styles share a very important focus: attention to the learning process. Both fields implore educators to understand as thoroughly as possible how people learn. Both fields of study also acknowledge the complexities and uncertainties of a full understanding of the learning process, and they recognize that a theory about learning is the basis of many educational decisions. In a very practical way, teachers who are interested in their own learning process, reflective about their unique ways of learning, and curious to understand their own brains will bring valuable perspectives to their work with learners in the classroom.

Implications and Applications

Tentative recommendations for applications of brain research to the classroom are amazingly consistent. Among the ones that support accommodation of diverse learning styles are:

- Full and in-depth study of content is very important. It creates connections for students among content areas and connections between content and their personal lives and experiences.
- Emotional connections should be made through explicit choices of methods and sensitive processing of learning.
- The integration of emotion and logic is a natural function of the brain and should be a natural function of curriculum.

- Active engagement and processing is more stimulating for the brain than passive experiences.
- Seeking and creating meaning is the most valuable part of learning. This has to be done in a personal and active way by each learner.
- Holistic, entire pieces of content, can and should be learned together even though the process might initially be messy or may seem unsequential to an outsider.
- The curriculum should be rich with challenges and stimulating content. Students can learn more than we currently offer them.
- The physical environment must be carefully orchestrated and must support exploration.
- It is essential to have an emotional climate of enough challenge without threat, which the Caines call "alertness."

Another important implication is that studying brain research will give us deeper and more sophisticated explanations for successes and problems we continue to see in schools. For example, in the last 15 years we have seen that cooperative learning is successful for many students. Understanding the social aspect of the brain and the learning style needs of social learners helps us implement cooperative learning more carefully. We also know that the best way to teach reading to all students is neither phonetics nor whole language—but an approach that is responsive to the student's learning style. Understanding brain research and learning styles explains this fact and can help us to be more intentional in our approaches to teaching reading.

Most important, the connection of brain research and learning styles concepts will be immensely important to students who are not currently successful in school. "As educators begin to explore the full potential of the brain," says Michael Grady (1990), "they will find ways to assist students, who in the past may have been considered slow, unmotivated, apathetic, or to have other kinds of learning problems" (p. 11). A serious understanding of the learning process is long overdue in the practices of our schools. Brain research makes tremendous contributions to this understanding.

5

Thinking About Style

One of our greatest mistakes as educators and politicians is not perceiving that our "here" is the student's and the people's "there."

—PAULO FREIRE

What are the roots of our current schooling practices? In *The Third Wave*, futurist Alvin Toffler (1981) says that every civilization is guided by a hidden code that runs through all its activities. He points out that our society is most familiar with the principle of "standardization," which is a common notion in education: "[T]o prepare youth for the job market, educators designed standardized curricula. Men like Binet and Terman devised standardized intelligence tests. School grading policies, admissions procedures, and accreditation rules were similarly standardized" (pp. 47–48).

Closely related to standardization is another principle that Toffler calls synchronization: "Pupils were conditioned to arrive at school when the bell rang, so that later on they would arrive reliably at the factory or office when the whistle blew . . . . Children began and ended the school year at uniform times" (p. 52).

Acceptance of the principles of standardization and synchronization, part of the array of social forces that affect the curriculum, may logically lead educators to search for a standard model of schooling to serve the needs of all students. This search extends to identification of a best method for teaching all students.

In the past few decades, these best methods have ranged from computer-assisted instruction to integrated curriculum and direct instruction. Each of these methods proves effective with some students—but produces little or no success with others. Standardized programs may achieve some measure of effectiveness, but if one accepts the fundamental existence of personality style, then the best that could be hoped for with any standardized program is success limited to students who either possess the style implicit in the program's design or have mastered the ability to style flex and adapt to any program.

The standardization and synchronization in our educational system stem from the fact that it was developed within a highly industrialized society. This impact of society cannot be ignored. Because our society has changed, education must follow suit.

Style As an Approach to Education

In the past few decades, the word *style* has been popular in the lexicon of education. It appears in various combinations (learning style, teaching style, administrative style) in such documents as state education standards, K–12 textbooks, and college and university faculty handbooks. There are a multitude of style-related resources, including audiotapes, videotapes, and teacher education texts.

In some ways, it would be disingenuous to decry this development, for it indicates the dissemination of research and information about styles concepts. Educators' increased familiarity with learning styles would seem to evidence that a movement away from standardization is well under way. On the other hand, it also may be a cause of some concern. Recognition of style-related words does not necessarily signify adequate understanding of the concepts and certainly does not mean educators have taken the necessary steps toward implementation.

A graduate student who also teaches recently observed: "Learning style is what you older [sic] people studied. Younger educators are into multiple intelligences." Her comment was not isolated, but reflects our experience that many school districts want somebody to "consult" about multiple intelligences and are generally adamant that their faculties already "know about" learning styles. This raises the question whether a comprehensive title like "style" and the active recognition of individual differences as applied to learning can go "out" of fashion. What exactly does this student's statement mean, especially because individual differences in learning are well proven in educational and psychological research? Isn't multiple intelligences also a theory about individual differences? What is it that districts hope to accomplish with their faculties through their professional development offerings? Does one abandon the body of research and work about styles that preceded Gardner, or, as we would argue, include Gardner as a contributor to the theory of individual differences applied to learning and his work as another excellent opportunity for educators to actively recognize individual differences in the classroom? These are questions that must be considered if we are to end the search for a "standardization" of educational theories that stands in direct contradiction to what a body of research about individual differences tells us.

Theories of style have the power to change the status quo by focusing educational decisions on the individual person. Much of schooling is designed to "cover" material. Knowledge of style puts the focus on the meaning that each individual gleans from the material. Evolution toward this concept would involve teachers and students in a dynamic system of education that would have acceptance of individual differences as its base.

This framework does not automatically lead to new models or programs to replace old ones. It is a fundamental change in attitude. Current models and programs will be retained when and as they are appropriate. Understanding the needs of the individual will be the guideline. This attitude will frustrate those who seek a standard answer to questions of learning, but many educators already know, as Mackenzie (1983) reports in his review of effective schools research: "In the buzzing complexity of a school environment, imprecise answers may be precisely the kind to be sought. When a formula gives the appearance of great precision, it is almost surely going to be wrong" (p. 13). This acceptance requires maintaining or developing an attitude that puts understanding and active recognition of the needs of the individual in the forefront of educational theory and methodology.

An Educator's Philosophy and Experience

Kohn observes that "the overwhelming majority of teachers . . . are unable to name or describe a theory of learning that underlies what they do in the classroom, but what they do—what any of us does—is no less informed by theoretical assumptions just because these assumptions are invisible. Behind the practice of presenting a colorful dinosaur sticker to a 1st grader who stays silent on command is a theory that embodies distinct assumptions about the nature of knowledge, the possibility of choice, and what it means to be a human being" (Kohn, 1993, p. 10).

Whether it is clearly articulated or not, every educator operates from a particular philosophical stance regarding the process of education. If their personal philosophy does not value individual differences, the research and data on styles will not have meaning for an administrator or teacher. A recognition of individual differences must be basic to an educator's philosophy if theories of style are to be used successfully.

Educators must hold that the concept of styles is an attitude or an approach that is brought to the education process. Theories of style do not provide a new set of techniques that constitute yet another standardized methodology; rather, all the theories presented in this book, including Gardner's, are an approach to reconsider and enhance the theoretical basis for methods already being used. Given the pragmatic nature of education, sooner or later any theory must "degenerate" into the application of that theory. As Ira Shor (1992) aptly puts it: "Knowing is power only for those who can use it to change their conditions" (p. 6).

Educators bring practical experience to their jobs, and they should draw upon that experience as they seek to apply research on styles. In most instances, an experienced teacher has discovered certain methods that work effectively in the classroom. To implement concepts of styles, a teacher need not be asked to give up these methods or even to change them drastically. Styles theories should supplement what teachers already use and help them systematize their knowledge of the individual ways people learn.

As you reflect on the information about style presented in this book, you are undoubtedly giving the theories personal meaning. This interpretation, formed from both your personal philosophy and your experience, provides a framework for your decisions on how to use the theories of style.

Educators who have at their philosophical core a firm belief in the individual and the need for ongoing recognition of individual differences remain actively engaged in accepting the challenges that are implicit in actively acknowledging these differences in the classroom. This engagement is profound and important, transcending the faddish quality of certain educational movements, for it strikes at the very heart of what it means to be a person. Given the solid foundation of educational and psychological theory and practice that styles theory rests upon, pervasive and long-lasting effects should be seen not only in the progress of the individual student but in the changes that take place within education as a whole in order to honestly accommodate all those students, teachers, and administrators in the system.

The danger in having "learning styles" prescribed as part of a larger context for education is that the underlying principles can begin to narrow to a single program. The implementation of learning styles principles is not like "doing" thematic units or whole language. The former represents a broad research and philosophical base that undercuts the core of synchronization and standardization and opens up the schools to freely explore constructivist principles. The latter are techniques that can fall within the broader context of application of "styles." That the difference between the above may not be noticed, and that "styles" may fall into the category of "techniques," lessens the power that styles represents. The theories can fall prey to what Theodore Roszak (1972) described as "the suave technocracy [which] knows how to accommodate much divergence— but without significantly redistributing power or changing the direction of main line social policy" (p. 44).

One cannot set styles theories apart from the context of the educational system within which they operate. Nor is it realistic to set out to change the system through the advancement of an idea or set of theories. But as Roszak warns us, attention must be paid to the ability of the educational system to continue to move forward with its emphasis on standardization and synchronization while appearing to accommodate the contradictory forces that implementation of learning style theories carries. A "suave" system can best be challenged through careful reflection on theories that underlie recognition of individual differences and the day-to-day application of those theories in the school classrooms. Bringing together your personal framework with the theories of style to form an approach to education can be explored philosophically by comparing the process to existential psychology.

Existential Psychology

Existential psychology has its roots in the work of the Danish philosopher Soren Kierkegaard and the German philosopher Friedrich Nietzsche. Rollo May (May et al., 1958) builds on their work to express his thoughts about the existence of the person.

> *The term "existence," coming from the root ex-sistere, means literally to stand out, to emerge. This accurately indicates [an attempt] to portray the human being not as a collection of static substances or mechanisms or patterns but rather as emerging and becoming, that is to say, as existing. For no matter how interesting or theoretically true is the fact that I am composed of such and such chemicals or act by such and such mechanisms or patterns, the crucial question always is that I happen to exist at this given moment in time and space, and my problem is how I am to be aware of that fact and what I shall do about it.* (p. 12, italics in the original)

By placing the emphasis on the person's existence, existential psychologists are able to speak about the person in a specific way.

> *The term the existential therapists use for the distinctive character of human existence is Dasein. . . . Composed of sein (being) plus da (there), Dasein indicates that man is the being who is*

there and implies also that he has a "there" in the sense that he can know he is there and can take a stand with reference to that fact. (p. 41, italics in the original)

In his book *Existential Psychotherapy*, the psychoanalyst Irvin Yalom (1980) expands on the preceding notion when he states that, *"Dasein is at once the meaning giver and the known. Each dasein therefore constitutes its own world; to study all beings with some standard instrument as though they inhabited the same objective world is to introduce monumental error into one's observations"* (p. 23, italics in the original).

The existential psychologist recognizes the person as dasein, and therefore in "being there" that person is responsible for taking a stance toward the world, a world that is not the same to each individual. Recognition of this uniqueness characterizes the existential position regarding therapy. Existential psychology *"is not a system of therapy but an 'attitude toward therapy.'* Though it has led to many advances of technique, it is not a set of new techniques in itself but a concern with the understanding of the structure of the human being and his experience that must underlie all techniques" (May, 1969, p. 15, our italics). Thus, the existential movement in psychology "does not purport to found a new school as over against other schools" (May et al., 1958, p. 7). It is a call to recognize that the client is unique regardless of the therapeutic method being used.

While the above is a brief discussion of certain existential principles, it does introduce ways that the existential attitude can be applied to a focus on styles in the field of education.

Existential Education

Yalom's (1980) statement quoted above, that "to study all beings with some standard instrument as though they inhabited the same objective world is to introduce monumental error into one's observations" is useful as one reflects that a similar monumental error would be committed in teaching all beings "as though they inhabited the same objective world." Theories describing style can be a check to prevent this error. All of the different theories have in common two basic thrusts: a recognition of a person's individuality and an attempt to provide the means to act upon that recognition.

Very few educators would blatantly state they do not recognize individual differences. Therefore, it makes little sense to speak of a "learning styles teacher" as opposed to a "traditional" or an "open concept" teacher. In a sense, every teacher is "existential" and "learning styles oriented" to the extent that he or she is an effective teacher. Many educators will find in the various theories of styles a systematizing of what they already know: that people are different in how they perceive, think, feel, and act. Consequently, all aspects of education must recognize these differences. An effective educator responds to differences whether the school setting is traditional, open, or alternative.

This fact should not oversimplify the complexities involved in teaching 20 to 35 individual students in a classroom at one time. Teaching involves hundreds of immediate "decisions that require artistry—a fine, swift, intuitive sense of situations" (Hunter, 1979, p. 45). Styles can, however, provide some basis for the swift sense of a situation by helping the teacher focus on the individual.

In the classroom the teacher is also dasein, and the teaching process is a reciprocal relationship between teacher and learner. "The interchange between a teacher and her pupils will be different every moment, and the teacher must be prepared to react to each child in terms of the unique question, idea, problem, and concern that he is expressing at that particular instant" (Combs, Avila, & Purkey, 1971, p. 5).

The teacher receives information necessary to refine the act of teaching and can alter that teaching based on feedback from the student. In similar fashion, the student receives feedback from the teacher and can adjust his or her learning. Both teacher and student are learning. The error of overemphasizing methods or programs leads to a focus on the method rather than on the person who constructs meaning from the method. Approaching learning with styles in mind is something the teacher does *with* students and not *to* them.

Gerald Kusler (1982), an educator who works with theories of style, says: *"Great chunks of the research support a simple dictum:*

know yourself, know your students, believe in what both can do. Because of cognitive and learning style work we can know ourselves and our students in a way that counts—as learners and thinkers" (p. 14, italics in original).

Educators must borrow from the existential psychologists the view that the concept of styles is an attitude or an approach that is brought to the education process. Theories of style do not provide a new set of techniques that constitute a standardized method of style but, rather, an approach to methods already being used. This is not meant to rule out the fact that new practices or methods may emerge from a study of styles, but these should not be the primary focus in education using style.

6

Defining Style

The Drum
daddy says the world is
a drum tight and hard
and i told him
i'm gonna beat
out my own rhythm

—Nikki Giovanni

To understand people's behaviors, we need to look at the roots of their actions. One way to do this is to consider several basic ways in which we all interact with a situation, a person, information, or ideas. First we take in the occurrence; then we think about it, react to it, and ultimately act upon it. These basic functions guided us to create four categories of style differences.

- Style is concerned with cognition: People perceive and gain knowledge differently.
- Style is concerned with conceptualization: People form ideas and think differently.
- Style is concerned with affect: People's emotional responses and values differ.
- Style is concerned with behavior: People act differently.

These categories help organize the diverse aspects of style, but they are not meant to be rigid. The complexity and subtlety of human behavior makes any organization of individual differences accurate in one instance but arbitrary in the next. To understand styles and their implications for education, it is best to view these categories in conjunction with all the characteristics that are integrated in the total personality of each human being.

Cognition: How Do I Know?

Perception, the initial stage of cognition, involves receiving, obtaining, taking possession of, and discerning information, ideas, and concepts. Some of us best perceive what is real; others clearly see possibilities with their imaginations. Some people see parts of a whole, separating ideas from their context, while others see the whole, not unlike the difference between seeing the forest or the trees.

These perceptual differences affect what and how something is received. My best intentions and extensive efforts to convince another to see exactly as I see will not eliminate these personal differences. A gifted artist can describe the gestalt of a painting, but some viewers will be struck by, and confined to, a single image in the work. The artist can plead, cajole, and discuss the entire painting in detail, but to little avail if the viewer's perception governs a certain view.

Consider how it would be if you hiked through the woods with a friend who suddenly became fascinated with a mushroom. At first, you might not even see the mushroom; your friend must point it out. Then, even when you physically see it, it doesn't mean the same thing to the two of you. You never eat mushrooms, and besides, you're on the hike mainly to enjoy your friend's company. But your friend is an accomplished gourmet chef who is looking to a new challenge: learning to cook with wild mushrooms he himself gathers. He'll soon be taking a class to learn to distinguish between edible and poisonous varieties. Your perceptions about the mushroom, obviously, are different.

Two people listening to the same music respond differently to the nuances of the sound, reflecting the depth of their musical experiences and their personal perceptions. Perhaps one is tuned to certain subtleties, while the other listens more generally. Two people sitting next to each other at a movie will recall different things when they discuss the film later. Students in a class often hear the teacher's directions in very different ways.

Gaining knowledge is another part of cognition. People get information in different ways. Some people use abstract sources, reading about things and listening to others' descriptions. Others need concrete experiences. The concrete person[1] often will depend directly on the senses for information: "I see it; now I know what it is." The abstract person is more receptive to secondhand sources of knowledge. Some people have to touch something or see it operate before they accept it as real, while others can imagine a vivid reality without needing to experience it. There are also sensory specialists, those people who rely on one sense more than another to gather information. Again, these different ways of getting information and gaining knowledge reflect distinct personal styles.

Conceptualization: How Do I Think?

People also exhibit differences in what they do with the knowledge they gain: how they process information and how they think. Some people are always looking for connections and ways to tie things together. Others are more divergent: One thought, idea, or fact triggers a multitude of new directions. Some people order ideas, information, and experiences in a linear, sequential way, while others organize their thoughts in clusters and random patterns. Some people think aloud; they verbalize ideas as a way of understanding them. Others concentrate on understanding concepts and experiences privately in their own minds. Some people think quickly, spontaneously, and impulsively; others are deliberate and reflective.

We see these and other examples every day. You may have had the experience of asking someone, "Whatever made you say that?"

---

[1] It is important to distinguish between styles and developmental stages. Those who research style do not address themselves directly to the concrete stage of acquiring knowledge but say that at any age—whatever the developmental level—some people are more or less concrete in their style, relative to their appropriate stage of development.

Then you realize the person was thinking about something in a very different way than you were. The important point is that these differences form patterns for each person and affect their total behavior.

Affect: How Do I Decide?

Differences in motivation, judgments, values, and emotional responses also characterize individual style. Some people are motivated internally; others seek external rewards. Some people actively seek to please others: children to please their parents and teachers, adults to please bosses and spouses. Some people simply are not attuned to others' expectations, and still others will rebel against any such demands. Some people make decisions logically, rationally, objectively, and coolly. Others decide things subjectively, focusing on their own and others' perceptions and emotions. Some people seek frequent feedback on their ideas and work; some are crushed by slight criticism. Others welcome analytical comments, and still others would never ask an outsider for a critique.

For some people, the medium is the message; others focus directly on the content. Some people are emotionally involved in everything they do, and others are neutral. The emotional learner prefers a classroom with a high emotional energy while another learner works best in a low-key environment. These affective differences are also stylistic and interrelated with the conceptual and cognitive characteristics discussed above.

The discussion of differences in affective style does not contradict basic humanistic beliefs in education. Everyone does best in a supportive atmosphere free from excessive criticism. But an awareness of stylistic differences can help administrators and teachers recognize that every person does not seek the same affective response and understand the kinds of support students, parents, and coworkers want.

Behavior: How Do I Act?

Cognitive, conceptual, and affective patterns are the roots of behavior, and pervasive and consistent stylistic characteristics will be reflected in a person's actions. The reflective thinker, for example, can be expected to act in a reflective way in a variety of situations from decision making to relating to people. Some people scan a situation to get the overall gist before tackling a problem; others focus on a certain part of the problem immediately and start with it. Some people approach a task randomly; others are very systematic. Some people need explicit structure; others prefer and perform best in a more open-ended situation. Some people prefer to work alone, and others like groups. Many people prefer working in certain kinds of physical environments.

In education, we recognize a variety of differences in how people learn and how these basic styles affect the individual learner's behavior. Reflective students are slow to respond to questions and need to think through a response carefully. Impulsive learners respond quickly and blurt out their thoughts. The step-by-step person learns best when each stage is clear and the transitions are spelled out. Another kind of learner makes intuitive leaps. After several weeks of struggling with division of fractions, this student may suddenly announce, "I've got it!" This same intuitive learner also will be impatient with sounding out parts of a word and doing phonetic worksheets when she has already grasped the essence of a story.

In sum, people differ in the ways they perceive, think, feel, and behave. Researchers have identified many specific examples of these differences, as summarized in Figure 6.1, and these theories are discussed in the following chapters. Equally important, the personal and professional experiences of educators provide constant evidence that style differences exist and that they affect many aspects of learning and teaching each day.

FIGURE 6.1

FOUR ASPECTS OF STYLE

Category	Characteristics*	Researchers
COGNITION perceiving, finding out, getting information	sensing/intuition	Jung; Myers-Briggs; Mok; Keirsey and Bates; Hanson, Silver, and Strong
	field dependence/field independence	Witkin
	abstract/concrete	Gregorc, Kolb, and McCarthy
	visual, auditory (verbal, musical), kinesthetic, tactile	Barbe and Swassing, Dunn and Dunn, Gardner
CONCEPTUALIZATION thinking, forming ideas, processing, memory	extraversion/ introversion	Jung, Myers-Briggs, Keirsey and Bates
	reflective observation/active experimentation	Kolb and McCarthy
	random/sequential	Gregorc
	logical intelligence	Gardner
AFFECT feelings, emotional response, motivation, values, judgments	feeling/thinking	Jung; Myers-Briggs; Mok; Keirsey and Bates; Hanson, Silver, and Strong
	interpersonal, intrapersonal	Gardner
	effect of temperature, light, food, time of day, sound, design	Dunn and Dunn
BEHAVIOR manifestations of all the above-mentioned characteristics		

* Characteristics separated by a slash (/) indicate bipolar or opposite traits.

7

A Brief History of Style

Let A be some experience from which a number of thinkers start. Let Z be the practical conclusion rationally inferable from it. One gets to the conclusion by one line, another by another; one follows a course of English, another of German, verbal imagery. With one, visual images predominate; with another, tactile. Some trains are tinged with emotions, others not; some are very abridged, synthetic and rapid, others, hesitating and broken into many steps. But when the penultimate terms of all the trains, however differing *inter se*, finally shoot into the same conclusion, we say, and rightly say, that all the thinkers have had substantially the same thought. It would probably astound each of them beyond measure to be let into his neighbor's mind and to find how different the scenery there was from that in his own.

—WILLIAM JAMES

The eminent American psychologist, philosopher, and educator William James wrote those words in *The Principles of Psychology* more than a hundred years ago. It seems that what we today call

61

"style" has long been a concern of psychologists and educators seeking to describe an individual's many facets.

Early Work with "Style"

It is not clear who first used the term *style* in this way. The Greek physician Hippocrates identified Sanguine, Choleric, Melancholy, and Phlegmatic personalities. For most of this century, research on individual differences has been conducted primarily in the field of psychology. German psychologists explored individual cognitive style differences at the turn of the century. Perhaps best known among them is Carl Jung (1921/1971), whose articulation of "psychological types" first appeared in English in 1921.

The word *style* is used in American psychologist Gordon W. Allport's work in the 1930s, when he defines consistent patterns appearing in individuals. Allport (1937/1961) notes that interest in individual differences in psychology "grew up at the beginning of this century" and that "many psychologists would consider this movement as coextensive with the psychology of personality" (p. 15). Many of these personality theories are based upon studies that were conducted regarding perception: *"Perception is the point of reality contact, the door to reality appraisal, and there is no doubt that here especially are the selective, adaptive controls of personality brought into play"* (Klein, 1951, pp. 328–329, emphasis in the original). A look at several experiments carried out at this time illustrates the importance that psychologist Klein placed on perception as "the point of reality contact."

Diminishing Research

In 1945, Lowenfeld reported a distinction between visual and haptic types, with the former experiencing the world primarily through vision and the latter primarily through touch. In his tests he discovered that one person in four depends upon touch and kinesthesis rather than vision.

In work he did during the late 1940s and early 1950s, Klein (1951) found that "a person continually brings to bear in any kind of situation what for him are 'preferred' ways of meeting reality"

(p. 336). Whereas Lowenfeld spoke of preferences in terms of visual and haptic types, Klein speaks of levelers and sharpeners: "[The] leveling group followed a pattern which we called 'self-inwardness' and emphasized a retreat from objects, avoidance of competition or of any situation requiring active manipulation. [The sharpening group] defines people who generally find competition and exhibitionism congenial, who have high needs for attainment, who energetically and oftentimes aggressively push themselves forward, and who have a great need for autonomy" (p. 336).

Herman A. Witkin began his work on perception in the late 1940s and continued it until his death in 1979. Witkin, Moore, Goodenough, and Cox (1977) proposed the existence of different perceptual tendencies in persons depending on how they view and use their surroundings. Witkin spoke of two poles of cognitive differentiation as field-dependent or field-independent. In tests designed to determine reliance on cues received from the background field, if "the performance range perception is strongly dominated by the prevailing field, that mode of perception was designated 'field-dependent.' At the other extreme, where the person experiences items as more or less separate from the surrounding field, the designation 'field-independent' was used" (Witkin et al., 1977, p. 7).

Allport (1937/1961) defines cognitive style as "distinctive ways of living in the world" (p. 271). Before 1955, psychologists had identified several classifications of people who illustrated Allport's "distinctiveness"—including the designations visual/haptic, levelers/sharpeners, and field-dependent/field-independent, all discussed above.

Unfortunately, research into individual differences gradually diminished. Leona Tyler (1965) attributes this decline to the fact that because "tests of this sort showed very little relationship to school success, the enthusiasm of psychologists for the whole mental test movement was considerably dampened. Because tests of the kind that Binet and Henri had been recommending, tapping complex intellectual characteristics rather than perceptual sensitivities, stood up better under this kind of evaluation, they set the pattern for later work, and the attempt to measure perceptual differences was largely abandoned" (p. 212).

In other words, school success, measured in terms of good grades, could be proven to relate to a student's IQ. A high IQ indicated the potential for a high grade. On the other hand, in overall terms, a field-dependent student did not do better or worse in school than a field-independent student. Whereas it was "better" to have a high IQ rather than a low IQ, it could not be proven that it was better to have a certain perceptual sensitivity. In terms of school success, style by itself was neutral.

As research psychologists lost interest in the topic, there was little or no communication between education and psychology regarding individual differences. Educators were either not aware of the cognitive style research or ignored it, ". . . *partly because many of the studies were conducted in fields other than education, and partly because educators . . . have emphasized programs rather than individual learning styles*" (Dunn and Dunn, 1975b, p. 44, emphasis in the original). "Therefore in both education and psychology, the possibility that the world might actually look, sound, and feel differently to different persons, that they might solve problems and form concepts in quite different ways, and that the same stimulating situation might carry different meanings for them was something investigators did not generally take into account" (Tyler, 1965, p. 211).

Current Style Inquiry

Since the late 1960s, educators have directly addressed the "possibility" cited above by Tyler. Anthony Gregorc (1982a) speaks of different mind qualities, describing how we take in and process information. Rita Dunn and Kenneth Dunn (1975a) have investigated a number of learning preferences, which they organize by categories called stimuli. Several applications of Carl Jung's original identification of psychological types have been made for education, and the identification of modality sensitivities has been studied by a number of educators. Howard Gardner (1983) focuses on individual potential by describing multiple intelligences.

With these educators' identification of various patterns of perception, processing, feeling, and behavior, classroom implications and applications were immediately described. The Dunns focused on the importance of accommodating each student's learning style, developed an assessment tool for diagnosis of the preferences, and prescribed strategies and accommodations for matching learning style to instructional techniques, structures, and environment. Gregorc was most interested in self-knowledge, and he designed ways for people—especially adults, teachers, and administrators—to understand their own styles and bring that knowledge to their interactions with students who would inevitably be both similar and different in style.

As the various researchers shared their work, different perspectives and applications became evident. Additionally, the work on learning styles began to expand, and more researchers and practitioners entered the field. Kathleen Butler (1984), who studied initially with Gregorc, brought her experience as a teacher to the work and designed an instructional model that suggested diverse approaches for learners of different styles and also differentiated among levels of thinking based on Bloom's work. Her contribution added a depth to curriculum development. Marie Carbo (1982), a reading specialist who studied with the Dunns, immediately applied learning style theories to reading instruction. Her work suggests that teachers match reading instructional strategies with the students' preferred way of learning to read.

Bernice McCarthy (1980) brought several learning style and brain researchers together for a conference and formed her 4MAT model from a synthesis of concepts. As a practitioner herself, she wanted an immediately usable system for teachers to apply to curriculum design and instruction. Gordon Lawrence (1982/1993) continues to articulate educational applications of Jung's work, and Robert Hanson, Harvey Silver, and Richard Strong have used Jung's theories to form their own model of learning and teaching style. They have been particularly attentive to combining style perspectives with other issues in education such as higher-level thinking skills and various assessment techniques.

Howard Gardner (1991) addressed educational applications of his multiple intelligences theory in *The Unschooled Mind.* Further applications of his work for the classroom have been suggested by a variety of authors. (These key models are described in more detail in Chapters 8–14.) Educators now regularly draw on the fields of psychology and neurobiology to expand their awareness of individual differences. Studies of brain functioning and its relationship to learning continually intrigue teachers and administrators and stimulate broader approaches to curriculum and methods of instruction. Interest in the potential of the human mind has brought fascinating theories and challenges to schools.

Through these various approaches, education is now actively engaged in understanding and recognizing individual differences. This movement is profound and important. In his introduction to a collection of papers on research in style and brain behavior, James Keefe (1982) says: "Knowledge about learning styles and brain behavior is a fundamental new tool at the service of teachers and schools. It is clearly not the latest educational fad. It provides a deeper and more profound view of the learner than previously perceived and is part of a basic framework upon which a sounder theory and practice of learning and instruction may be built."

This current focus builds upon a solid foundation of theory and practice in both psychology and education. A solid research base, and continuing study, confirms, illuminates, and elaborates the theories of style. Additionally, many useful books give specific guidelines and examples for classroom application. The resources are available; the challenge is to study enough theory to make the applications sensitive and appropriate.

In a 1995 article discussing some of the myths arising from application of the theories of multiple intelligence, Gardner observed that multiple intelligence theory "is in no way an educational prescription" (p. 206). While he states that educators are best suited to create applications of his theory, he also describes concerns about naive applications: "I cherish an educational setting in which discussions and applications of MI have catalyzed a more fundamental consideration of schooling. . . . Such examination generally leads to more thoughtful schooling" (p. 209).

Claxton (1990) summarizes this notion well: "The study of learning styles and different ways of knowing may be less important for what it tells us about learner differences (as important as that is) than for what it tells us about effective education for all students. In doing so, they make an important contribution to the teaching profession generally and to the students we seek to serve" (p. 8).

Part II

Examples of Style

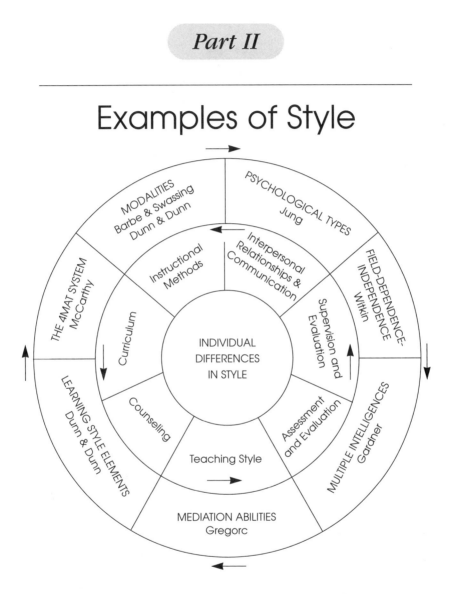

The next seven chapters illustrate several areas in education that are affected by individual differences in style. In discussing each area, we describe a specific study of style. The "match" we have made between a model and an application is intended as only one *example* of use of specific research on style. As the wheel above is rotated, it is clear that each model of style can contribute to each area of implementation.

8

Interpersonal Relationships and Communication:

Jung's Psychological Types

"First of all," he said, "if you can learn a simple trick, Scout, you'll get along a lot better with all kinds of folks. You never really understand a person until you consider things from his point of view . . . "

"Sir?"

" . . . until you climb into his skin and walk around in it."

—HARPER LEE
To Kill a Mockingbird

Mrs. Hand comes to school for the annual parent teacher conference and asks Mr. Day, the teacher, how Darren is doing this year. "Darren has completed all of his assignments," Mr. Day responds, "and he regularly hands in his work. He is doing solid work for this grade." Mrs. Hand seems puzzled at this response and comments, "Yes, yes I know, I see his work when he brings it home, but I want to know how he is getting along with the other students."

In the classroom next door, Mrs. Mott asks the teacher, Mrs. Keble, how her daughter Sue Anne is doing this year. The teacher enthusi-

*astically responds that Sue Anne seems to be getting along with every-
one very well. At this point, in frustration, Mrs. Mott says, "Yes, I know
she has friends; she's always gotten along quite well. I want to know
about her schoolwork."*

When parents ask, "How's my child doing in school?" what do they
mean? As Mr. Day, Mrs. Kehle, and all teachers know too well, they
mean different things. For Mr. Day, getting along with other kids may
be of secondary importance, but when Darren's mother asks how he
is doing, she is asking about interpersonal relationships, not academics. For Mrs. Mott, her daughter's academics are her primary concern. These different intentions are all too familiar to people who
work in schools.

Clear communication and successful interpersonal relationships
are at the core of educational decisions and programs. When people
get along and understand one another, schools work well. Research
into effective schools has labeled this "positive climate," and an
extensive study of successful schools in England called it "positive
ethos" (Rutter, Maughan, Motimore, & Ouston, with Smith, 1979). To
explore the relationship of style to interpersonal relationships and
communication, we will discuss the work of Carl Jung.

Jung's Psychological Types

Philosophers and psychologists throughout history have won-
dered why people behave in different ways. In 1921, Carl Jung offered
an extensive explanation of behavior patterns in the book *Psychological Types*.

Jung proposed that to understand different behaviors we should
focus on the basic functions people perform in their lives. He said
that every psychologically healthy human being operates in a variety
of ways depending on the circumstances, people, and situation. Despite situational adaptations, each of us inevitably will develop comfortable patterns that lead us to behave in certain predictable ways.
Jung used the word "types" to identify these personality styles.

One basic function all psychologically healthy human beings
perform is perceiving concepts and experiences. Jung identified two

ways of viewing people and situations. Some people see the world through their senses: vision, hearing, touch, and smell. They observe what is real, factual, and actually happening. They stick to what they see, and for them, seeing is believing. Because of the emphasis on the pragmatic, real, and observable aspects of perception, Carl Jung called this function "sensation." This function enables each of us to observe accurately, gather facts, and focus on practical actions.

Another way of viewing the world has to do with possibilities and relationships. This way of seeing experiences and people helps us to read between the lines, attend to meaning, and focus on what is intended and what might be. This part of perception helps us to read subtleties, body language, tones of voice, and cues that interpret the experiences of the senses. It leads us to look at old problems in creative and original ways. This kind of perception Jung called "intuition" because we focus on and react to meaning our minds create.

Jung explained that everyone uses both kinds of perception when dealing with people and situations, but we each tend to have a preference for one way of looking at the world. The kind of perception we favor most often becomes the window through which we observe life. Because these ways of looking at the world are fundamentally different, it stands to reason that if we are more likely to search for reality and facts through our senses, we are less likely to depend on and to trust possibilities, imagination, and intuition. Obviously the opposite holds true: Intuition leads us to search beneath and beyond reality and to distrust surface information. Our experiences tend to reinforce our way of looking at the world. We are most in tune with people who approach life the way we do, and sometimes we are confused and baffled by people who don't see what we see.

Jung also described another fundamental difference among people: Individuals approach the decision-making process in different ways. Some of us analyze information, data, situations, and people and apply a logical and rational process to making a decision. We pride ourselves on being objective, calm, cool, and collected. If the decision is difficult, we search for more information. We are deliberate and careful in our analysis of data because accuracy and thoroughness are very important. This process of decision making leads us to trust objectivity, facts, logical predictions, and rational arguments. When we arrive at a conclusion, we are confident that all alternatives have been explored and weighed against one another and that the final decision has been reached unemotionally and carefully. Jung described this function as the "thinking" function.

On the other hand, some of us approach a decision through a subjective, perceptive, empathetic, and emotional perspective. We search for the effect of the decision on ourselves and others. We consider alternatives and examine evidence to develop a personal reaction and commitment. We view the decision-making process as complex and somewhat subjective. Essentially, we see circumstantial evidence as extremely important. We live in a world of gray rather than black and white, and often we use the phrase "it depends" to describe the subjective nature of a decision. We will sometimes go against the tide of rational evidence because of some personal perception about a situation or person. Jung called this the "feeling" function.

Jung explains that every healthy human being uses both thinking and feeling in the decision-making process, but we each become more comfortable, and more skilled, in arriving at a decision in either a thinking or feeling way. Again, these functions are opposites on a continuum. Making decisions with an emphasis on logic and reason leads to a distrust of emotions, empathy, and personal perceptions. At the same time, a trust in perceptions and personal insight and values can lead to a skepticism of logic and rational evidence.

An important part of Jung's explanation of these four basic human functions was his insistence that no direct value was attached to one's approach to perception or decision making. Accurate, clear, and important perceptions can be gained through both sensation and intuition. Successful, effective, and rational decisions can be made through logical thinking and also through personal feelings. A mature approach to life includes a recognition that we need to use both kinds of perception and both kinds of judgment, each for the right purpose. Also, we need one another's strengths because "the clearest vision of the future comes only from an intuitive, the most practical realism only from a sensing type, the most incisive analysis only from a thinker, and the most skillful handling of people only from a feeling type. Success for any enterprise demands a variety of types, each in the right place" (Myers, 1962, p. 5).

The differences in approach become patterns for us and tend to affect all aspects of our personal and professional behavior. Because people see and think about the world differently, it is not surprising, Jung concluded, that patterns of behavior will be different for people who favor each type.

Another dimension Jung described was the extent to which our behavior is determined by our attitude toward the world. Jung said that many of us operate comfortably and successfully by interacting with things external to us: other people, experiences, or situations. Others are most interested in the internal world of their own minds, hearts, and souls. Jung described these differences among people as "extraversion and introversion." Again, he said every psychologically healthy human being functions in extraverted ways at times and in introverted ways at others, but we develop consistent patterns that are typical and comfortable. Some of us like to test our thoughts and ideas through talking or doing, until they become clearer to us. Others like to mull over thoughts and actions, reflecting upon them until they become more valid. Those of us who tend toward extraversion often think aloud. Those of us who operate more comfortably in an introverted way are pensive, reflective, and slow to act because we aren't ready to translate internal thoughts to the external world.

Jung found that the four functions of sensation, intuition, thinking, and feeling will be expressed differently by those with extraverted preferences and those with introverted preferences. An extraverted feeling person would be outwardly emotional and expressive, whereas an introverted feeling person would be reflective and private about emotions. But both would base a final, successful decision on the subjective aspects of an issue. Again, Jung was careful to describe the equality of both extraversion and introversion. He also recognized the problems that may arise when people of opposite kinds of expression communicate and work together.

These four functions and two types of expression provide the basis for Jung's descriptions of human behavior. He believed that we are each born with a tendency toward a particular pattern and that change in human behavior, while possible, is a very slow process. He believed that growth and maturity help us to develop our own strengths and also to understand other approaches to life.

73

Applying Jung's Theory

Carl Jung's theories have been adopted and applied by a variety of researchers throughout this century. When his book was translated into English in the 1920s, Katharine Briggs became interested in the concepts as they applied to her family and the people she knew well. She and her daughter, Isabel Briggs Myers, explored Jung's theories with their family and friends. They became convinced that Jung's work had wide application and tremendous potential for increasing human understanding. Seeing the need for personal understanding of the theories, they developed an instrument that would permit people to learn about their own type. Originally piloted in the 1940s, the Myers-Briggs Type Indicator (MBTI) has become a well-known and well-respected psychological instrument (Myers & Briggs, 1943/1976). Through forced-choice questions and word pairs, people can measure their own balance of intuition versus sensation, of thinking versus feeling, and of extraversion versus introversion.

As Briggs and Myers worked with Jung's theories, they became convinced of another important dimension. They believed there is a preference in each individual for the "judging" function or the "perceptive" function. Therefore, they added another continuum to their instrument. The desire to be open ended and to explore life is labeled "P" for perception, and the desire to bring closure and to regulate life is labeled "J" for judgment. Thus, their final instrument includes four continuums. The combination of the four scores produces 16 different types, as seen in Figure 8.1.

The Myers-Briggs Type Indicator is used extensively by human resource professionals, psychologists, counselors, those in religious life, and, more recently, educators. The Murphy Meisgeier Type Indicator for Children (1987) is an assessment tool for students. The Center for Application of Psychological Type publishes many books, monographs, and training materials and also reports extensive research, some dealing with education. Gordon Lawrence's book (1982/1993), *People Types and Tiger Stripes, A Practical Guide to Learning Styles,* suggests practical applications for teachers.

In the 1970s, psychologists David Keirsey and Marilyn Bates (1978) described their experience with the MBTI in a book called *Please Understand Me, Character and Temperament Types.* They

74

FIGURE 8.1

MYERS-BRIGGS DIMENSIONS AND TYPES

Extraversion (E) _____ Introversion (I)

Sensing (S) _____ Intuition (N)

Thinking (T) _____ Feeling (F)

Judgment (J) _____ Perception (P)

ISTJ	ISFJ	INFJ	INTJ
ISTP	ISFP	INFP	INTP
ESTP	ESFP	ENFP	ENTP
ESTJ	ESFJ	ENFJ	ENTJ

---

made another adaptation when they simplified the 16 labels into four basic temperaments by clustering the dimensions. They named these temperaments after the Greek gods Apollo (intuition and feeling), Prometheus (intuition and thinking), Epimetheus (sensing and judging), and Dionysus (sensing and perceiving). From Keirsey and Bates' basic temperament descriptions, educator Keith Golay (1982) developed applications for the classroom, which are described in *Learning Patterns and Temperament Styles*.

Another application of Jung's work has been made in industry by a management consultant named Paul Mok (1975). Working with the four functions of sensing, intuiting, thinking, and feeling, Mok described communication patterns associated with each function. His work focuses on the importance of understanding these communication patterns in relating to clients, in working effectively as management teams, and in diverse applications such as marketing, sales, and personnel.

With Mok's model as a basis, educators Anita Simon and Claudia Byram (1977) identified the importance of communication patterns for teachers working with students, parents, administrators, and one another. In their book *You've Got to Reach 'Em to Teach 'Em*, they describe the importance of knowing one's own style; of knowing how to style flex; and of applying a knowledge of students' styles to instruction, discipline, parent conferencing, motivation, rewards, and evaluation.

J. Robert Hanson, Harvey Silver, and Richard Strong used Jung's typology to develop learning and teaching style applications for education. They publish assessment instruments, research reports, and practical books for teachers. They have been particularly successful describing the importance of attending to style differences in various education efforts such as developing higher-level thinking skills, integrating curriculum, and comprehensive staff development. A 1997 article by Silver, Strong, and Perini describes ways to integrate learning styles and multiple intelligences, especially in assessment. The continuing work of these and other researchers and practitioners makes the original theories of Carl Jung easily available for educators to understand and use.

Communicating with Style

What happens at a school when people recognize differences in style and are willing and able to deal with them? First and foremost, diversity of human personality is accepted as the norm. Administrators, teachers, students, and parents are expected to be different. When we expect people to be different, we tune-in to people's assumptions about issues, problems, and questions. We ask, "How would Dale approach this?", "What will David think?", "How would Sandy solve this problem?", "What would be best for this student?"

Perhaps more important, we stop the futile search for the one right answer to educational issues and problems. There cannot be one best way to run schools, a right way to design a report card or a teacher evaluation, a best reading text for every student, a best physical design for a classroom, or, of course, a best way to teach. When we accept diversity as the norm, we recognize that things that work extremely well for some students, teachers, administrators, and parents will not necessarily work best for others. This is a fundamental change in thinking. Roland Barth (1980) described this challenge in the story of his job as principal of a public elementary school: "Diversity is abundant and free. Used wisely, deliberately, and constructively, it offers an untapped, renewable resource available to the public schools. We should learn to use it well" (p. 16).

Perhaps one of the most important applications of style awareness in human relations is the self-knowledge that we gain by recognizing our own perspective on the world. We begin to consciously identify our strengths and use the skills they give us. At the same time, we identify our weak areas and acknowledge the importance of compensating for them by changing our own behavior or collaborating with other people. Developing self-awareness without the judgmental labels of right, wrong, best, or better can produce a positive sense of self-esteem. As professional educators we respect the variety of approaches that colleagues bring to the teaching-learning situation, and we learn from them, but at the same time we are most comfortable with the skills our own strengths give us. Teachers and administrators in our classes and workshops often say that the best part of learning about style is knowing that "it's okay to be myself in the classroom."

In schools where diversity is accepted and taken seriously, conscious style flexing is practiced every day. Style flexing implies knowing not only your own style but your impact on others. Educators with a strong thinking pattern, for example, should know that some people see them as too attentive to detail, too bogged down in nitty-gritty facts, and very slow to come to decisions. Some colleagues will value that accuracy and exactness; others may see it as being extremely fastidious and picayune. Some will value thorough planning; others will see it as being rigid. A teacher may value his or her objectivity and control over emotion, but another person may see that as being cold and impersonal. Knowing that differences in style affect not only our own behavior but how others see us helps us understand how to better communicate with people.

When we understand others' styles, we can use our own and others' strengths to work together for the best results. What this implies, of course, is some modification of our own behavior but not necessarily a change in basic beliefs or philosophy. Instead, it is a conscious adaptation of behavior to facilitate positive communication.

Another example of style flexing at work is at a conference between an administrator, a teacher, and a parent to address the issue of remedial help for a student. Assume that the parent exhibits a strong feeling style and focuses on the emotional effect this decision will have on the child. When the parent comes from this perspective, it will not be helpful for a teacher to refer to test scores and go through a careful analysis of the child's achievement evaluations. Nor will it be helpful for the administrator to show comparisons illustrating the child's standing in relation to the rest of the class. What the parent needs to discuss most is the emotional impact the decision is going to have on the child. Both the teacher and administrator can help the parent focus on the academic areas as they relate to the child's emotional well-being. Comments such as, "It must be hard for Trisha to have to struggle academically," and "Trisha often seems to feel tense during tests" are going to be much more appropriate and helpful than comments directly related to objective data.

In this example, the best decision for the child will be made when the parent, teacher, and administrator communicate positively. The child will benefit by the collective wisdom of these people with their different perspectives on the problem. The decision to recommend special assistance for this child should include an analytical review of achievement as well as consideration of the emotional impact.

In this kind of situation, and the many others that occur every day, an understanding of the diversity of human nature and an acceptance of it as the norm can result in a cooperative attitude toward decisions and problems. Schools that celebrate diversity among people will be able to use this strength to produce effective learning.

9

Supervision and Evaluation:

Witkin's Field-Dependence-Independence

A trifling matter, and fussy of me, but we all have
our little ways.

—EEYORE TO POOH
From *The House at Pooh Corner* by A. A. Milne

"Good job, Kathy," Len Lubinsky, the principal, comments after drop-ping in on Kathy's language-arts class.

Later that day, Kathy is talking with her friend and fellow teacher, Gordon. "Good job! Can you imagine? What kind of com-ment is that? And he just dropped in! I wonder if he thinks this will count as an official observation?"

"Relax, Kathy," Gordon responds, "that's Len—he often drops in. It's his way of keeping in touch. I like those visits; they take the pres-sure off the 'official' observations. Be complimented that he said 'Good job!' He means it."

When teachers and administrators talk about supervision and evalu-ation, they bring their own set of values to these concepts. For some administrators supervision and evaluation are ongoing functions related to all their interactions with staff. These administrators feel that their role as instructional leaders includes a pervasive, low-key, continual supervision of staff. Other administrators pride themselves on the separation of evaluation from other interactions with staff. They carefully schedule evaluative observations and stick to specific objective criteria. In the final analysis, various approaches to supervision and evaluation will work if the administrator is skilled at whatever approach he or she takes. But the approach—the style—will elicit a different reaction from different staff, as illustrated above with Kathy and Gordon's comments.

Teachers, too, bring their own styles to issues of supervision and evaluation. Some prefer the casual drop-in approach; others want a formal schedule. Some value specific criteria in a checklist form. Others rebel at this approach, asking, "How could those lists capture the real strengths of my teaching?"

Again, the issue is not one of right or wrong but a matter of style. If teachers want an administrator to drop in regularly to get a sense of the positive climate of their classes, which they work hard to develop, that will be more important than the comments about an observation of a specific math lesson. But a teacher who feels that specific instructional skills are the most important indication of competency will want the administrator to formally evaluate a lesson. Comments about the students' relationships with one another in this class will simply not be as important.

Administrators and teachers need to be aware of these style differences in approaches to, and expectations of, supervision and evaluation. High expectations can be held for all staff, but because skill and style are not the same, competencies can be successfully demonstrated in various style ways. To discuss a specific example, we will focus on the cognitive style dimension of field-dependence-independence described by the late Herman A. Witkin and his colleagues. As you read, remember that other style models could as easily be applied to this important area and that the Witkin model has many applications to other areas of education.

Field-Dependence-Independence

Can you find the isolated figure in the more complex figure in Figure 9.1?

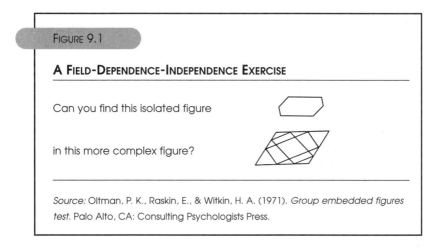

FIGURE 9.1

A FIELD-DEPENDENCE-INDEPENDENCE EXERCISE

Can you find this isolated figure

in this more complex figure?

Source: Oltman, P. K., Raskin, E., & Witkin, H. A. (1971). *Group embedded figures test.* Palo Alto, CA: Consulting Psychologists Press.

It takes some people less than three seconds to perform the task, while others, with similar intelligence, search for several minutes and cannot locate the isolated figure. What about you?

People vary in their abilities to differentiate objects from their backgrounds. This difference in perception can be extreme: A highly differentiated, field-independent person will quickly find the figure, whereas an extremely field-dependent person often needs to have the figure pointed out. Most of us lean toward one or the other of these poles; we differ in the time it takes us to complete the task and the complexity of problems we are able to solve. This perceptual characteristic of field dependency, originally labeled cognitive style, has been linked to learning, teaching, and many other behaviors.

The above figure, and others like it, are included in the Group Embedded Figures Test (Oltman, Raskin, & Witkin, 1971), which is derived from the work of Herman Witkin. In the latter half of the 1940s, Witkin and his associates began exploring distinctive perceptual characteristics among people. The researchers were interested in knowing to what extent a person's perception of an item was influenced by the context (field) in which it appeared. In other words, were there people who saw the tree while others saw the forest?

Early in his work, Witkin worked with the armed forces to determine why some pilots became disoriented and actually flew their planes upside down when they lost sight of the ground. To assess a person's perception of his or her own orientation in space, he devised an experiment in which the subject was seated in a moving chair, which was to be brought to true upright regardless of the slant of a small "room," framed in light, surrounding the chair. Similar experiments were conducted in which the subject was to locate a rod upright in the space of a frame. Both rod and frame could be tilted independently and were lighted while surrounding darkness eliminated other visual distractions.

These and other experiments led Witkin and his associates to define two extreme indicators of the extent to which the surrounding organized field influences an observer's perception of an item within it. A person with a field-dependent (FD/global) mode of perception is strongly influenced by the prevailing field, while the field-independent (FI/analytic) person experiences items as more or less separate from the surrounding field. Thus, the field-independent person is successful in attaining a correct upright placement of the chair and the rod in the above experiments by ignoring the surrounding room or frame. A field-dependent person, however, will align the chair or the rod more in relationship to the external clue (room or frame) and insist that it is upright. Most subjects tested scored along a continuum from FI to FD, tending toward one or the other pole.

Later, Witkin and his colleagues (1973) expanded the studies into different aspects of personality. They explored what the people clustering together near each pole have in common. Can people with FD and FI perception be expected to have certain consistent characteristics? Over time, Witkin and his associates became convinced that the field-dependence-independence dimension influences one's perceptual and intellectual domains as well as personality traits such as social behavior, body concept, and defenses. The results of more than 35 years of research, providing a rich and useful font of information, are compiled in bibliographies listing over 2,000 studies (Witkin et al., 1973).

Because Witkin's concern was primarily psychological research, educators have to examine his work thoughtfully to develop ways it can be applied properly to the educational setting. A solid research base exists for the field-dependent-independent concepts, but a wider knowledge and application of Witkin's work within educational circles is lacking. Witkin recognized the importance of his research for educators and prepared an extensive article on this aspect of his work (Witkin, Moore, Goodenough, & Cox, 1977). We compiled information from this article and adapted it for educational applications in the descriptions of learners in Figures 9.2 and 9.3.

Diagnosis of adults and students for field-dependence-independence is now possible with validated paper-and-pencil instrumentation. One of these instruments, the Embedded Figures Test (Witkin, 1969), is administered individually and takes about 30 minutes. Another instrument that has been widely used is the Group Embed-

---

FIGURE 9.2

HOW STUDENTS LEARN

Field Dependence	Field Independence
Perceive globally	Perceive analytically
Experience in a global fashion, adhere to structures as given	Experience in an articulated fashion, impose structure or restrictions
Make broad general distinctions among concepts, see relationships	Make specific concept distinctions, see little overlap
Have a social orientation to the world	Have an impersonal orientation to the world
Learn material with social content best	Learn social material only as an intentional task
Attend best to material relevant to own experience	Interested in new concepts for their own sake
Seek externally defined goals and reinforcements	Have self-defined goals and reinforcements
Want organization to be provided	Can self-structure situations
More affected by criticism	Less affected by criticism
Use spectator approach to concept attainment	Use hypothesis-testing approach to attain concepts

---

FIGURE 9.3

HOW TEACHERS TEACH

Field Dependence	Field Independence
Strong in establishing a warm and personal learning environment, emphasize personal aspects of instruction	Strong in organizing and guiding student learning, emphasize cognitive aspects of instruction
Prefer teaching situations that allow interaction and discussion with students	Prefer impersonal teaching methods such as lecture and problem solving
Use questions to check on student learning following instruction	Use questions to introduce topics and following student answers
More student-centered	More teacher-centered
Provide less feedback, avoid negative evaluation	Give specific corrective feedback, use negative evaluation

---

ded Figures Test mentioned above. This instrument is valid for ages 11 and above and can be administered to a group in 20 minutes. There is also a children's version of the instrument for youngsters between the ages of 5 and 10 (Karp & Konstadt, 1971), and a preschool version for children 3 to 5 years (Coates, 1972).

Witkin's work has a variety of messages for educators. His studies have consistently demonstrated cognitive styles to be independent of intelligence, and thus "field-dependence-independence appears to be more related to the 'how' than to the 'how much' of cognitive function" (Witkin et al., 1977, p. 24). Because cognitive style is neutral, both field-dependent and field-independent people, according to studies, make good students and good teachers. However, because style does affect success in specific kinds of situations, educators must be sensitive to style-related demands in teaching and learning.

In offering advice to educators for responding to cognitive style differences, Witkin and his colleagues urge us to consider the advantages of both matching and mismatching. He points out that the "development of greater diversity in behaviors within individuals seems as important an objective as the recognition and the utilization of diversity among individuals" (p. 53). Ultimately, he wants knowledge of field-dependence-independence to contribute to teachers' and students' abilities to use their own style strengths and then develop more diverse strategies to facilitate success in learning.

Style-Sensitive Supervision

What does this mean in terms of supervision and evaluation? As we've studied personality characteristics associated with Witkin's style patterns and talked with teachers and administrators about their styles, we've been able to develop some generalizations about supervision and evaluation. Figure 9.4 represents some typical expectations that teachers of different styles have for administrators. Figure 9.5 identifies some general concerns about evaluation. As with all

---

FIGURE 9.4

WHAT TEACHERS EXPECT FROM AN ADMINISTRATOR

Field Dependence	Field Independence
To give warmth, show personal interest and support	To focus on tasks and established goals
To provide guidance, to model	To allow independence and flexibility
To seek their opinions in making decisions	To make decisions based on analysis of the problem
To like them	To be knowledgeable about curriculum and instruction
To have an open door	To maintain professional distance
To "practice what they preach"	To be professionally experienced in appropriate content areas
To use tones and body language to support words	To give messages directly and articulately

---

Figure 9.5

How Teachers Want to Be Evaluated

Field Dependence	Field Independence
With an emphasis on class climate, interpersonal relationships, and quality of student-teacher interaction	With an emphasis on accuracy of content, adherence to learning objectives, and assessment of learnings
With a narrative report and personal discussion	With a specific list of criteria
With consideration of student and parent comments	With consideration of academic achievement and test scores
With recognition of effort and motivation	With evidence and facts to support comments

---

dichotomous lists, there is seldom a pure fit, but most people identify more with one style than the other.

What happens in a school that attends to style in the areas of supervision and evaluation? First and foremost, the people involved understand one another in a more realistic and profound way. A teacher knows "where an administrator is coming from" when he or she says "good job." A principal hears a teacher's "Just drop in any time!" with a deeper understanding. This mutual awareness can help focus the supervisory and evaluative process on professional growth.

At the same time, awareness of style will help educators respond to one another's needs in evaluation and supervision. An administrator will understand that some teachers need specific time commitments for evaluative visits and clear objective criteria. Others may want and need a casual observation schedule with more focus on the less tangible aspects of teaching, such as climate, student relationships, and motivation. When administrators and teachers understand one another's needs, they can use the supervisory process to take advantage of one another's strengths.

Understanding style in relationship to supervision can help administrators and teachers accept the value of multiple criteria for evaluation. They can consciously focus on the objective parts of instruction and curriculum and on the more subjective affective areas. As specific competencies are identified, multiple indicators of the competence, appropriate for various styles, also can be spelled out. One teacher might demonstrate organization in a linear way with a very neat plan book while another teacher might demonstrate organization by an ability to manage a complex integrated curriculum project.

At the same time, wise administrators and teachers will encourage diversity in the methods that are used in supervision and evaluation, seeking opportunities for clinical supervision, peer coaching among staff, objective-based checklists, and narrative reports. In his proposal for differentiated supervision, Allan Glatthorn (1984) urges that "teachers should have some choice about the kind of supervision they receive—in contrast to the situation that prevails in most schools" (p. 1).

Finally, supervision and evaluation that actively consider individual needs of the people involved can foster true professional growth rather than mandated procedures. It is always easier to accept suggestions from those with whom we share mutual respect. If we hear another's comments from the perspective of a different set of values, it is difficult to internalize them for our own growth. On the other hand, when someone seems to "understand me," I am more willing to accept his or her perspective. This openness helps me to listen, so that I really hear and can incorporate the suggestions in my professional work.

Educators who value individual differences must model that value in relationships with one another. Teachers and administrators who respect one another's styles can help one another improve through the supervisory process.

10

Teaching Style:

Gregorc's Mediation Abilities

Understanding one's own magical mystery is one of the teacher's most important assets if he is to understand that everyone is thus differently equipped.

—BUCKMINSTER FULLER

The Schimmels just moved to town, and today they are visiting the elementary school their children will attend. The principal, Mr. Areglado, welcomes them and gives them a schedule for their various classroom visits. After several hours, they return to his office, feeling generally positive about the school. But they are confused about the teaching differences they saw in each classroom. They ask Mr. Areglado to tell them more about the school.

He begins by explaining that the school's basic philosophy is to meet the needs of all children and to provide the best programs possible to help each child succeed. The Schimmels couldn't agree more, but still don't understand the differences in each classroom. Mrs. Schimmel asks, "Aren't there some basic rules about good teaching that guide the school?"

"Yes, of course," Mr. Areglado answers. "Our school believes in respecting and encouraging diversity among the teaching staff. This

better helps them meet the needs of individual students. Let me tell you about some of the teachers to give you an example.

"Mrs. R. is the senior member of our staff. She has been teaching here for more than 20 years. She's warm, personable, and caring, and these qualities are immediately apparent in her relationships with the children and in the atmosphere she sets in her classroom. She personalizes her curriculum by focusing on the interests of her students and sharing her own interests. Children and parents respond enthusiastically to her as a person, and children are successful in her room.

"Mr. D. across the hall is one of the newest teachers on our staff. He is a very active, project-oriented person. He has a lot of hobbies and is very skilled with his hands. He'll often build curriculum materials for the children to use, and he encourages them to do active projects to express their learning. He has the ability to make abstract ideas real for children and to relate learning to their everyday lives. Parents often find themselves roped into projects to help him and the children work on curriculum. The bottom line, of course, is that through active involvement in projects, children develop their skills.

"Down the hall you visited our team-teaching classroom. Mrs. S. and Ms. J. have been working together for the past three years. They enjoy this arrangement because they find that sharing the curriculum gives them an opportunity to become expert in a few areas. Ms. J. handles all of the reading, and she's marvelous at coordinating a variety of approaches to help the children learn to read. Several years ago she finished her master's degree in reading, and she continues to update herself regularly by taking courses at the local university. I've seen some children gain several years in their reading skills under her guidance. Mrs. S. is equally enthusiastic about mathematics. She can make children excited about math skills as well as concepts. Best of all, of course, these two teachers plan the curriculum together, and they use their skills to complement each other.

"I could go on about all of the other members of the staff. The point, Mr. and Mrs. Schimmel, is that we have a very strong, yet very diverse, staff. Our parents have come to enjoy that aspect of our school, and they look forward to their children encountering different approaches as they move through the grades. Why don't you tell me a

*me a little bit more about your children and what you hope for them
so that I can recommend an appropriate placement?"*

Teaching Style

Could this scenario work in today's schools? Can a school successfully educate children by allowing and even encouraging a great
deal of diversity among its staff? Is it possible that this might even be
the best way to run a school? Roland Barth (1980), a former principal believed so, and described his experiences in *Run School Run*:
"I have found that when teachers are teaching in ways consonant
with their own personal style and professional philosophy, both they
and their students appear to benefit" (p. 15).

When we accept that people really are different, we also must
accept that teachers will bring their own unique qualities to the way
they teach. We call this "teaching style," and it means we will see
teachers' personalities reflected in their professional behavior. We
will see differences in the way teachers relate to students. We will
see differences in how teachers structure and manage their classrooms. We will see differences in the mood and tone that teachers
set in their classrooms. We will see differences in the methods and
materials teachers use to help students learn. We will see differences
in curriculum interests and emphases. We will see differences in expectations for student work and in priorities and strategies for evaluating student learning. All of these are manifestations of a teacher's
individual style.

Teaching style governs the reality of the classroom. No two
teachers will use a program or text in exactly the same way. Each
teacher personally makes the curriculum come alive for students.
John Goodlad (1984) calls the teacher "coach, quarterback, referee,
and even rule-maker" (p. 108). In his extensive study of schools he
found that

> the classroom is indeed the teacher's domain, and here, ac-
> cording to our data, teachers perceive themselves to be quite
> autonomous. Our teachers saw themselves to be in control of
> what they taught, and how. . . . . Approximately two-thirds of
> the teachers at all levels perceived that they had complete

"control" in their selection of teaching techniques and students' learning activities. (Goodlad, 1984, pp. 188–189)

When we accept that teaching styles exist and that the individual teacher has a great deal of autonomy, we then have to decide to encourage or discourage individual styles, to inhibit diversity or encourage uniformity. We need to decide when teachers must be similar and when they can be different.

It is important to remember the difference between style and competence. Certainly there are specific, identifiable teaching competencies. For example, effective teachers need clear purposes and objectives. They must use effective instructional methods and techniques, motivate and support students in appropriate ways, monitor instruction, and assess and evaluate the effectiveness of learning. The question of teaching style is whether it is possible, and even desirable, for teachers to exhibit these competencies in a variety of individual ways.

In Ted Sizer's (1984) report on high schools, he describes three successful teachers and attributes their success to their judgment, which he sees as an extension of their personalities. "One visits classes and sometimes see experts, each with his or her own special style," he notes (p. 153). Sizer concludes his study with a number of imperatives for better schools. The first is: "Give room to teachers and students to work and learn in their own, appropriate ways" (p. 214). To further consider the subject of teaching style, we will look at the work of Anthony Gregorc.

Anthony F. Gregorc and Mediation Abilities

Gregorc says that his interest in style emanated from his own comfort and discomfort in a variety of jobs he held as teacher, administrator, and college professor. He also considered his practical experiences with students in a high school for exceptional children, where he and staff members observed an unevenness in children's successes.

The subjective personal experiences and objective professional experiences led Gregorc to identify and examine the notion of individual differences in an applied and philosophical way. This balance of the practical, philosophical, and psychological is apparent throughout this work, and it brings depth to his model. For Gregorc, the style reflected in our behavior is an indication of the qualities of our mind. He thus identifies style patterns in the context of a total view of life, which he calls the "Organon System."

> *The primary purpose of life is to realize and actualize one's individuality, spirituality, and collective humanness.* . . . The ORGANON system is an organized viewpoint of how and why the human mind functions and manifests itself through the human personality. [It studies] two mediation abilities of the mind: perception and ordering. (Gregorc, 1982a, p. v, emphasis in original)

When we perceive, our mind "sees" things in a mental, symbolic, intuitive, and emotional way and also "sees" things in a realistic, direct, and physical way. These different kinds of perception—abstract or concrete—describe opposite ends of a continuum (Figure 10.1). Every person is capable of using abstract and concrete perception, but we each have a tendency to prefer one over the other.

The mind also exhibits an ability to order information, knowledge, ideas, and concepts. Sometimes it orders things in a linear, step-by-step, and methodical way. At other times, it orders in a nonlinear, tangential, and leaping way. These two kinds of ordering, sequential or random, form opposite ends of a continuum (Figure 10.2). While every person can use both sequential and random ordering, we each have a tendency to prefer and to operate more frequently and more successfully with one kind of ordering.

Combining both perception and ordering, Gregorc identifies four distinct patterns of style. Some people will perceive in a concrete

---

FIGURE 10.1

PERCEPTUAL CONTINUUM

Abstract _____ Concrete

FIGURE 10.2

ORDERING CONTINUUM

Sequential _____ Random

---

way and order with a sequential pattern, thus exhibiting a Concrete Sequential (CS) style. Others will perceive in an abstract way and then order sequentially, resulting in an Abstract Sequential (AS) style. Some will perceive in a concrete way and then order in a random way, producing the Concrete Random (CR) style. And finally, those who perceive in an abstract way and order randomly will be identified as having an Abstract Random (AR) style.

The Gregorc Style Delineator (Gregorc, 1982b) is a self-analysis tool designed to assess a person's perceptual and ordering abilities. A person ranks sets of words, then a numerical score is obtained for each of the four patterns. These scores are plotted on a grid that produces a four-pointed shape (Figure 10.3). Strong preference for one

---

FIGURE 10.3

SCORING GRID FOR GREGORC'S STYLE DELINEATOR

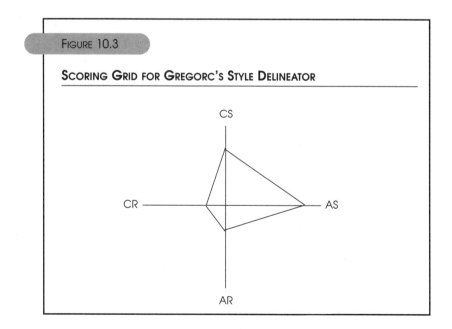

93

style over the other three will produce a very dramatic point toward that part of the grid.

The resulting visual picture of the relationship of the four style scores is very effective for seeing how there is always an interaction of different style characteristics in our behavior. A person with a dominant AS style and a strong CS backup style would have a profile similar to that shown in the example given in Figure 10.3.

Mediation Abilities and Teaching Style

Kathleen Butler, originally a doctoral student working with Gregorc, has developed extensive, practical applications of Gregorc's model for teachers. She realized that because of style differences, higher levels of thinking could not be described in the same terms for every person. Using Bloom's taxonomy, she described style differences for each level of thinking. Called Style Differentiated Instruction, her model for curriculum and instruction is both practical and challenging. She has continued to expand her work, addressing modality and multiple intelligence differences as well. She has published excellent materials with extensive, practical examples including full curriculum units and books for students to examine their own styles.

Butler (1984) defines teaching style in this way:

> Each teacher brings a unique self to the classroom. The strength of our personal goals, expressed through natural style, pulls in a fairly consistent direction and creates our view of what teaching can and should be. *Teaching style is a set of attitudes and actions that open a formal and informal world of learning to students. It is a subtle force that influences student access to learning and teaching by establishing perimeters around acceptable learning procedures, processes, and products. The powerful force of the teacher's attitude toward students as well as the instructional activities used by the teacher shape the learning/ teaching experience and require of the teacher and student certain mediation abilities and capacities. Thus, the manner in which teachers present themselves as human beings and receive learners as human beings is as influential upon the students' lives and learning as the daily activities in the classroom.* (pp. 51–52, emphasis in original)

Consider how the mediation abilities described in Gregorc's model will be reflected in a teacher's style. A teacher who prefers concrete perception and sequential ordering will exhibit the Concrete Sequential style. This teacher will be practical, use hands-on learning experiences, take field-trips, organize projects, and have a variety of manipulative materials available for students. When parents visit this teacher's classroom, they will see a utilitarian environment where schedules, fire-drill procedures, and the daily bulletin are posted. The teacher will expect students to be task-oriented and to complete their work by showing all the steps. The CS teacher appreciates specific order and routines and will manage the classroom in a structured and logical way. These teachers have special abilities to make school practical, realistic, predictable, and secure.

When a teacher perceives in an abstract way and then orders sequentially, he or she will have an Abstract Sequential teaching style. Teachers who prefer this style will apply their logical and sequential reasoning to abstract ideas and to symbols, theories, and concepts. They will encourage students to be analytical, evaluate what they are learning, and support their ideas with logical evidence and data. When families visit this teacher's class, they might see students doing research in an impersonal, structured setting. These teachers have a deep respect for depth of knowledge and expertise, and they will expect students to exhibit good study skills. Gathering accurate information is very important for learning in these classrooms, and students will use many abstract resources, especially books. These teachers are wonderful at encouraging students to be intellectually curious and to rigorously build a broad base of knowledge.

When a teacher perceives in an abstract way but then orders randomly, he or she will have an Abstract Random teaching style. Teachers who prefer this style rely on personal understanding of curriculum and content. They focus on individual students, their interests, and their needs. They design classroom experiences in a child-centered way. They respond perceptively to the moods and tones of the class and behave spontaneously when something of interest to themselves or the students occurs. They enjoy artistic and creative activities, projects, and materials. When parents visit this classroom, they will see children's work displayed along with colorful posters reflecting the teacher's and students' interests. These teachers see their job as educating the whole child. They strive to develop self-esteem and self-confidence, and they require students to cooperate and share. They make the content in the classroom personal and seek to suit the curriculum to the individual as much as possible. They focus on relationships by teaching knowledge and skills through themes. These teachers are often inspiring and help students bring joy and enthusiasm to learning.

Finally, a teacher who perceives in a concrete way and orders randomly will have a Concrete Random teaching style. Teachers who prefer this style emphasize practical, realistic work but want it expressed in original and creative ways. They encourage students to invent and problem solve by producing products that are both useful and original. These teachers are active, enthusiastic, flexible, and spontaneous. They are resourceful, use a variety of methods, change often, and, of course, promote active student involvement. They love to experiment, and they encourage students to make choices, think for themselves, and ask "Why?" Visitors will see a busy environment without an immediately apparent order and with students' work in various stages of completion. These teachers "challenge students to move beyond given knowledge and traditional learning to discover new ideas and products for themselves" (Butler, 1984, p. 107). They are wonderful catalysts, encouraging both students and fellow staff members to view learning as a constantly challenging adventure.

Within each of these descriptions of teaching styles we encounter individual diversity, because each teacher's primary style would be affected by strengths in other style areas. Still, on a visit to almost any school, examples can be found of each of these teaching styles.

Teaching with Style

Working with the concept of teaching style implies celebrating and using the diversity of teachers' differences. It means encouraging each teacher to work with his or her strengths and actively using the diversity among the staff in curriculum planning and schoolwide decision making; maintaining a balance of styles in staffing the school as a whole and in staffing individual departments and grade levels;

and respecting the notion of style in planning for growth for individual teachers and for improvement in the school programs.

A school that celebrates diversity of teaching style will encourage CS teachers in their practical structured approaches, will applaud AR teachers for their personal warmth and spontaneity, will be grateful for the enthusiasm and experimentation of CR teachers, and will welcome the intellectual rigor that AS teachers bring. In such a school, decisions about programs and organization will be made by using the strengths of these different styles.

Curriculum committees will be formed to consciously maximize the diversity, so that different perspectives will be brought to the final recommendations. Teachers will be encouraged to learn from one another while also respecting one another's differences. It will be accepted that students will respond to teachers in different ways, and student placement will take this into consideration. Matching a student with a like teacher will be done when appropriate, but at the same time students will be encouraged to grow and stretch by working with a teacher who is stylistically different from themselves.

Specific teaching competencies will be defined, and teachers will be encouraged to evaluate their competencies in light of their own styles. Growth will be expected from each teacher but without comparison with another person whose style is different. When each teacher, individually or in conjunction with a supervisor, plans for personal growth, particular style strengths and potential problems will be a key focus. The administrator will work with each person to validate strengths, to plan for ways to minimize weaknesses, and to develop new skills. CS teachers might be encouraged to develop a higher tolerance for spontaneity and to avoid being too inflexible in their expectations and structures. AS teachers could be urged to make learning practical and to value emotional responses from students. AR teachers could be asked to consciously acknowledge the importance of objective information in their teaching and assignments. And the CR teachers could be encouraged to maintain appropriate routines and respect proven traditions.

A school that uses and celebrates diversity in teaching style creates an opportunity for all students to find their styles accommodated at some time in various classrooms. Teachers will know that students can and do learn in different ways because they will see their colleagues using a variety of strategies to produce success for students. They also will be aware of the different models of teaching among one another enabling them to develop more diverse teaching strategies. Parents will see the school offering a variety of options for their children and will also know through practical experience that children can and do learn from different teaching approaches. Perhaps most important, because these teachers experience respect for their own individuality, they will in turn feel comfortable conveying this respect for uniqueness in their relationships with students.

11

Counseling:

Dunn and Dunn's
Learning Style Elements

Every child can be educated; it is only a matter of
the method of education.

–SHINICHI SUZUKI
Nurtured by Love

COUNSELING OFFICE, END OF FIRST QUARTER:

*Susan is in your office because she is not doing well in school. Not
doing well translates to a 1.3 grade point average out of a possible
4.0. She is a bit tense, sitting and fidgeting. After the preliminaries,
you get to the crux of the matter by asking Susan what she feels is
causing the difficulty with her schoolwork.*

"I have the ability, but I don't apply myself," she replies.

*With this reply two things may race through the counselor's
mind: Susan has been counseled before, and she just said what you
were going to say!*

*After reassuring her that what she said is indeed true, you en-
courage her to study harder and perhaps talk about the need for good
grades to keep from closing off options in the future. Then you send
her back to class.*

COUNSELING OFFICE, END OF SECOND QUARTER:

*Susan is in your office because she is not doing well in school. Not
doing well translates to a 1.3 grade point average of a possible 4.0.*

99

She is a bit tense, sitting and fidgeting. After the preliminaries, you get to the crux of the matter by asking Susan what she feels is causing the difficulty with her schoolwork.

"I have the ability, but I don't apply myself," she replies.

At this point the whole situation begins to seem vaguely familiar. Once more you reassure her that she does indeed have the ability, and you again tell her to study harder. Only this time there is an important difference: You say it louder and slower—almost in the same way you would give directions to a person who has difficulty understanding the language you are speaking.

Although the above scenario may sometimes be all too real, it is meant to exaggerate what often transpires in the counselor's office. How can we change this pattern?

Knowledge of styles may help open up a dialogue with students and lead them to view the counselor as part of a "learning team." It also can offer students like Susan concrete ways to improve their learning efficiency. It can encourage them to take tentative steps toward accepting responsibility for their learning. Knowing their individual styles helps students approach learning more efficiently and maximize their intellectual gifts.

The researchers we chose for this application example are Rita and Kenneth Dunn. The work of any of the researchers on style could appear in this section, just as the Dunns' model can be used effectively in other application areas.

Dunn and Dunn's Learning Style Elements

The Dunns are well known in the area of learning styles. They have published widely in education journals, written a number of books, and presented seminars across the country. The Dunns (1975a, p. 74) describe learning styles as "the manner in which at least 18 different elements of four basic stimuli affect a person's ability to absorb and to retain information, values, facts, or concepts." The four basic stimuli are environmental, emotional, sociological, and physical. The elements of each are illustrated in Figure 11.1.

To question students about these elements, the Dunns and statistician Gary Price developed a self-report instrument called the

---

FIGURE 11.1

RITA AND KENNETH DUNN'S LEARNING STYLE ELEMENTS

Stimuli	Elements			
Environmental	Sound	Light	Temperature	Design
Emotional	Motivation	Persistence	Responsibility	Structure
Sociological	Peers	Self	Pair	Team	Adult	Varied
Physical	Perceptual	Intake	Time	Mobility

Learning Styles Inventory (LSI). It is available in three different forms: grades 3–5, grades 6–12, and adult (called the Productivity Environmental Preference Survey, or PEPS).

Administration of the instrument is straightforward and convenient. For example, the person taking the grade 6–12 LSI answers 104 questions with one of five possible responses: strongly disagree, disagree, unsure, agree, or strongly agree. Some of the questions include:

- I study best when it is quiet.
- I like to make my parents happy by getting good grades.
- I like studying with lots of light.
- I concentrate best when I feel warm.

The responses are computer scored, and the results indicate which elements are important to a person's learning. With this convenient reference, a teacher can focus on the learning style of each student throughout the day and confirm or adjust the inventory profile with observations of actual classroom behaviors.

The computer scoring also can provide a group summary sheet. This allows teachers to quickly determine which students have certain learning style preferences without having to examine each student's individual profile. Common class patterns will emerge, and the teacher can adapt methods, physical environment, and groups. For example, the teacher can identify which students need quiet to learn and which prefer sound in the background. If the same students are always out of their seats, the LSI results probably will reveal a preference for mobility. Likewise, students who are "always talking" may very well be those whose LSI results indicate a preference for learning in a team or with a peer.

With careful study of the Dunns' model, a counselor, working with the teacher, can devise ways to meet the individual needs of students. At the very least, knowing students' learning preferences can make the teacher more sensitive to individual differences among students. This increased sensitivity will make it easier for that teacher to view some student actions, such as being out of the seat, as expressions of individuality tied to learning rather than a threat to authority or discipline. The teacher can then provide the student with a strategy that responds to this learning preference.

Along with the valuable information provided about the individual student, the practicality and ease of the administration and scoring of the LSI makes the Dunns' research appealing and has led to its wide use. Educators in many schools have attended inservice programs on the Dunns' model and, after administering the LSI, adapted their teaching to the results.

The Dunns complement the widespread application of their model with continued research in the area of learning style. Rita Dunn is a professor at St. John's University, New York, and the school has become a center for research on styles. In several surveys of the research (Dunn, 1982; Dunn, Beaudry, & Klavas, 1989, 1995), she and her colleagues cites studies confirming that

- Students can identify their own strong style preferences,
- Teaching through learning styles increases academic achievement and improves students' attitudes toward school, and
- Learning style is often stable over time and consistent across subject areas.

The Dunns and their associates also have developed curriculum materials and a variety of other resources for application in the classroom. Their training workshops guide teachers in a diagnostic-prescriptive process to develop strategies and materials for meeting the needs of each learner.

Marie Carbo has created a specific application of the Dunns' learning style model for reading. When she was a doctoral student working with Rita Dunn, Carbo brought her extensive experience as a reading specialist to the study of learning styles. She adapted the Dunns' Learning Style Inventory to reading, called it the Reading Style Inventory, and developed a variety of strategies to meet students' learning preferences in reading.

Carbo has challenged the overemphasis on phonics instruction, arguing that many students need hands-on and holistic approaches to learn to read. In a 1997 review of 20 years of reading styles work, Carbo reported, "[W]e know beyond a doubt that there is no single best way to teach every youngster to read . . ." (p. 38). Carbo's work can provide useful information for a counselor working with a student experiencing difficulty in reading.

Counseling with Style

With the Dunns' profile of learning style, a counselor has something of substance to begin work with students who aren't performing well in school. The counselor can prepare for an interview by studying the student's learning style printout. For example, the counselor in our scenario above knows that whatever Susan is doing to study is not working. It won't help to tell her to study harder and longer at her desk. This has not worked in the past, as evidenced by her stagnant grade point average. Telling Susan to study three hours a night when two hours is not working illustrates the "get-a-bigger-hammer" approach to problems. It ignores the student's unique needs and strengths.

Instead, the counselor might ask Susan to describe how she studies when she has something important to learn. Let's imagine she responds that she sits at the desk her parents bought her when she began high school and studies under a high-intensity light for two hours each afternoon, just before supper.

By reviewing the learning styles printout, the counselor knows that Susan prefers informal design, meaning she prefers to study on the floor, couch, or bed. She likes dim lighting where she studies. The LSI printout also reveals that Susan's best time to study is in the evening after supper and not in the late afternoon. Thus, by studying the Dunns' instrument and interviewing the student, it is possible to identify elements that actually are inhibiting Susan's ability to learn. She could be a more efficient student if she studied under low light while lying on the carpet, sometime after dinner.

Susan's profile might also reveal that she is not persistent. An experienced counselor will realize that a nonpersistent person cannot study for two straight hours each night. When the counselor asks Susan to describe what she does for those two hours at her desk, she answers that she spends the time in her room studying. But as the conversation progresses, she realizes that a good portion of the time is spent in other activities, such as reading magazines or writing notes to friends.

It would be more realistic at this point to ask Susan if she thinks she can study for 15 minutes, then take a break, and return sometime later for another 15 minutes. This may be more practical for her and enable her to begin to build on success instead of dealing with the frustration of attempting to study an impossible (for her) two hours in a row! The 15 minutes can be expanded gradually until Susan studies for longer and longer time spans.

Susan's case is only one example of the application of student learning styles to counseling situations. Knowledge of learning styles can establish a useful, systematic basis for counseling. The student interview allows for fine-tuning the results of the learning style assessment by letting the student personally verify the results. Students enjoy talking about how they like to learn. The problem is that they are rarely asked!

When students do discuss their learning, they affirm that they know how they prefer to learn, and they begin taking responsibility for their own progress. They also see that information about style is neutral in terms of intelligence. Helping students become more comfortable with their personal patterns of learning releases some of the tension many students feel about school and paves the way for improved learning and grades.

12

McCarthy's 4MAT System

Instruction begins when you, the teacher, learn
from the learner, put yourself in his place so that
you may understand what he learns and the way
he understands it.

—KIERKEGAARD

*Once upon a time in a town called Could It Happen, a young teacher
was hired to start a new school. The school board asked this teacher
to design the curriculum.*

If you were the teacher in this scenario, what would you present to
the school board? Where would you start, what would you do, how
would you build knowledge and skills, and what would you consider important?

For most of us, such questions are answered by someone else, or at
least we assume they are, and therefore we often don't take an active
role in examining these issues. Let's put ourselves in the shoes of the
young teacher in this scenario and explore some curriculum questions.

Curriculum Questions and Issues

What do we mean by curriculum? Do we mean the body of
knowledge that we teach and expect students to learn? Do we mean

the management of learning? Do we mean the applications of knowledge? Or do we mean all of the above?

Curriculum issues truly reflect diversity in thinking about schooling. For some educators, and for some of the general public, curriculum is a body of knowledge composed of facts, concepts, and skills that transmit societal and cultural values. People who define curriculum this way put energy into defining and describing what students need to know to become well-educated adults and good citizens. For other educators and citizens, curriculum should focus on the application of knowledge to develop skills needed for a successful professional and personal life. They ask what learners will do with their knowledge. Still others believe curriculum should mean the skills needed to learn; curriculum should be the process of learning to learn. They believe schools should teach processes of finding out, discovering, developing insights, organizing ideas, thinking analytically, and evaluating information. For them, the curriculum should inspire a love of learning.

While these perspectives are not mutually exclusive, the emphasis on different beliefs is reflected in the variety of work on curriculum and in practical decisions about content and process. In a review of the writing about curriculum, Decker Walker (1980) concludes that curriculum is a diverse and varied area full of mixed opinions, values, purposes, and content. "Practically everything known to humanity is relevant, importantly so, to the resolution of some curriculum problem. . . . Curriculum is clearly an iffy subject" (p. 76).

Another important and pervasive issue about curriculum is autonomy and control. Who makes the decisions, and who will be accountable to whom? Should the federal government be involved in setting national directions by deciding, for example, that there should be more emphasis on science education in the elementary grades or computer literacy at all ages? Should there be national standards for competence? Should a local community have the final decision about which books should be in the school library, which topics children consider in social studies, and the number of years of foreign language study required for graduation?

Should professional educators, administrators, and teachers have the most active role in the decision-making process? Should a local school staff identify and decide upon the knowledge, skills, and process that will be emphasized in their building? Should students be permitted, or even encouraged, to have a say in what they learn? What role should parents have in deciding what their children will learn?

Another pervasive issue in curriculum concerns its organization and management. To what extent are knowledge, concepts, and skills organized in a linear, building-block fashion? To what extent are themes and content relationships used to give meaning and context to learning? How much does a person need to know about something? Should a topic be studied in-depth, or is it better for learners to survey an area so they can be knowledgeable about a variety of things? Should curriculum be organized with careful attention to child development? Are students able to learn certain skills and information better at certain ages? How can the notion of individual styles guide some of these decisions? To consider many of these issues, this chapter focuses on the work of Bernice McCarthy and the 4MAT System of learning styles.

McCarthy's 4MAT System

Bernice McCarthy has taught at various grade levels and has been a counselor and teacher educator. Her own practical experience that students learn in different ways led her to conduct research on learning differences. In 1979, she received a grant from the Mac-Donald Corporation to bring together several leading researchers in learning styles and brain functioning. From the exchange of ideas among these experts she developed her own approach to defining and explaining individual differences in learning. She synthesized a variety of learning style models but settled on the work of David Kolb as an umbrella descriptor of the learning process and the different ways people learn.

In the early 1970s, Kolb, a management expert from Case Western Reserve University, developed an experiential learning model. He identified two major dimensions of learning: perception and processing. He said that learning results from the way people perceive and then process what has been perceived. He described two opposite kinds of perception. At one extreme are people who perceive through concrete experience, and at the other extreme are people who perceive through abstract conceptualization.

As he explored differences in processing, Kolb also found examples at opposite ends of a continuum. Some people process through active experimentation, while others process through reflective observation. The juxtaposition of the two ways of perceiving and the two ways of processing led Kolb to describe a four-quadrant model of learning styles (Figure 12.1).

Focusing on Kolb's work and integrating the work of other learning style researchers, McCarthy described four types of learners. In Kolb's upper right-hand quadrant, Quadrant I, Type One learners are those who perceive through concrete experience and process through reflective observation. In Quadrant II, Type Two learners perceive through abstract conceptualization and process through reflective observation. In Quadrant III are Type Three learners, those who perceive through abstract conceptualization and process through active

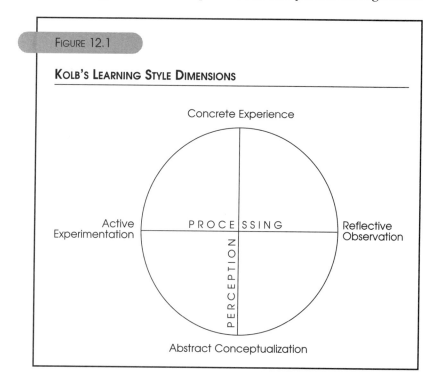

FIGURE 12.1

KOLB'S LEARNING STYLE DIMENSIONS

experimentation. In Quadrant IV are the Type Four learners, who perceive through concrete experience and process through active experimentation. Each of these learners, because of individual differences in perception and processing, develops a unique pattern to learning.

Research on brain functioning was another area of study that fascinated McCarthy, and she explored it further in the conference mentioned above. She was particularly interested in studies of hemisphericity and findings that the right hemisphere and left hemisphere specialize in certain kinds of tasks. This work led McCarthy to carefully consider each of her four types of learners and to explore how the right and left hemisphere would function for these unique learning styles. The final result was the imposing of the right and left specialization on each of the four learning styles, which she calls the 4MAT System (Figure 12.2).

Type One learners perceive in a concrete sensing/feeling way and process in a reflective/watching way. Their right hemisphere searches for personal meaning through an experience, and the left

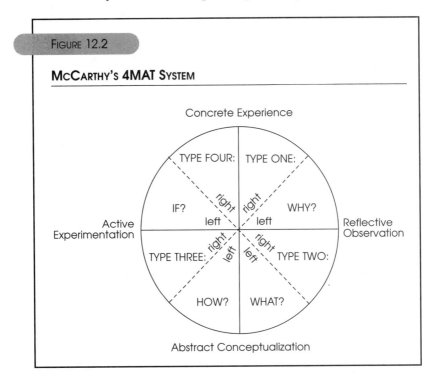

FIGURE 12.2

McCarthy's **4MAT** System

hemisphere seeks to understand an experience by analyzing it. In the effort to find personal meaning, such learners often ask "Why?" Type One learners must think about what they personally value and care about; they must understand how learning will affect them and how it relates to their beliefs, feelings, and opinions. They seek a personal reason for learning and knowing something.

Type Two learners perceive in an abstract and thinking way and again process in a reflective and watching way. For them the most important question is "What?" Their right hemisphere seeks to integrate experience with what they know and to clarify their need for more knowledge, while their left hemisphere seeks that new knowledge. Type Two learners want to get accurate information. They want to deal with facts and right answers, and they want to develop concepts and theories in an organized way. They care about exactness and detail, and they respect authority and expertise. For these learners, it is important to identify what can be known and to seek knowledge carefully and fully.

Type Three learners also perceive by thinking and abstracting, but they process by actively trying out and doing. For these learners, the most important question is "How does it work?" Their right hemisphere looks for an individual application and use of the learning, while their left hemisphere looks for more general examples of "What have other people done?" These learners want to be doing; they want to try and practice. It is this act of involvement that helps them test information in the real world and develop clear understandings. They seek to make things useful, and they value things that are practical and have a concrete purpose. They care about the general application of knowledge and about how they personally are going to use what they are learning.

Finally, Type Four learners perceive through concrete sensing and feeling and process by doing. These learners ask the question "If?" Their right hemisphere seeks to develop extensions of their learning, and the left hemisphere seeks to analyze the learning for relevance and significance. Type Four learners want to see relationships and connections between things; they want to be inspired to do things that are really important in life. They seek to inspire other people and are often catalysts who make others excited about the learning process.

They seek to synthesize skills and knowledge and personal meaning into something that creates a new experience for themselves and others. These learners understand and accept complexity.

McCarthy's 4MAT model describes the learning process as a natural sequence from the personal interests of Type One learners to the "if" questions of Type Four learners. McCarthy, adhering to Kolb's original model, believes that all learners—and all learning experiences—should start with Quadrant I.

> The 4MAT system moves throughout the learning cycle *in sequence*, teaching in all four modes and incorporating the four combinations of characteristics. The sequence is a natural learning progression that starts with the teacher answering—in sequence—the questions that appeal to each major learning style. (McCarthy, 1985, p. 62, italics in original)

At first, personal meaning and motivation are set for what is to follow. The next step is acquisition of the new knowledge and concepts, followed by practical application. The final step is the more complex synthesis and extension. Thus, for McCarthy, every learning experience should begin at Quadrant I and follow through the cycle to its natural conclusion in Quadrant IV.

Using this sequence, she believes that each learning style will have an opportunity to shine part of the time. All learners will be able to develop their own natural abilities when they are working in their own strongest learning style area. At the same time they will develop other abilities necessary to be good learners by working in other quadrants. "[T]o learn successfully, a student also needs expertise in other learning styles; together these styles form a *natural cycle of learning*" (McCarthy, 1997, p. 46, italics in original).

McCarthy emphasizes that what ordinarily happens in most schools is a very limited part of the eight-step process, concentrating primarily on the left quadrant for the Type Two learners and left quadrant for the Type Three learners. In other words, most schools deal with knowledge acquisition and general application. The 4MAT System brings much more depth to a learning experience.

To illustrate how her model works, McCarthy has developed a number of lessons at all levels from kindergarten through college. She shows that any content or process can be taught using her sequential eight-step system. To follow her lesson model, a teacher would begin in Quadrant I by creating an experience and then offering a way for students to analyze the experience personally. Then in Quadrant II, students integrate the experience and continue to analyze in a more conceptual way, actually developing new concepts. Continuing to Quadrant III, students practice with what is given, then make personal, practical application. Finally, in Quadrant IV, students synthesize by looking for something relevant and original, then they seek to apply what they've learned to more complex experiences.

When teachers are trained in this eight-step lesson model, they experience greater or lesser ease with different steps in the process because of their own learning styles. It is easier, for example, for a Quadrant I style teacher to develop activities that create personal meaning and experience. At the same time it is easier for a Quadrant IV teacher to develop experiences that extend into the realm of new ideas and relationships. Quadrant II and Quadrant III teachers are helped by commercial curriculums and texts that particularly address left mode experiences for acquisition of knowledge and the general practice of skills.

McCarthy has written several books to illustrate her model. The first, *The 4MAT System: Teaching to Learning Styles with Right/Left Mode Techniques* (1980), is a general description and an overview of her model that includes sample lessons. In 1983 she and Susan Leflar edited *4MAT in Action: Creative Lesson Plans for Teaching to Learning Styles with Right/Left Mode Technique.* This is a collection of lessons illustrating how the 4MAT System would work, with examples from primary grades to postsecondary schools and in diverse subject areas such as language arts, social studies, mathematics, and law. In 1985, she published *4MAT and Science: Toward Wholeness in Science Education* with Bob Samples and Bill Hammond (Samples, Hammond, & McCarthy, 1985). It illustrates how the 4MAT System would be exemplified in a total science program and also how specific science lessons can be taught through the 4MAT plan. All of these resource materials follow the same basic theme and description of the four-quadrant learners, and all emphasize a need for the sequential progress of learners through the eight-step learning experience.

McCarthy's company, Excel Inc., continues to publish materials for educators, including computer programs for lesson management. She established a sophisticated training program using school district personnel to bring the 4MAT approach to their own schools. Her materials offer both an immediate application to the classroom and the challenges of in-depth examination of curriculum and instruction.

For an assessment of an individual's learning style strengths, McCarthy uses David Kolb's Learning Style Inventory (1976). It presents groups of four words to be ranked. Numerical scores are computed for each of the four dimensions, and then the differences in scores on the perceptual and processing dimensions are calculated and plotted on a graph. Thus, a visual picture of one's placement in a particular learning quadrant is obtained. Kolb calls Type One learners "Divergers," Type Two learners "Assimilators," Type Three learners "Convergers," and Type Four learners "Accommodators."

Curriculum with Style

What would happen in a school that built curriculum based on knowledge of individual differences? In such a school, complex issues of content, purpose, control, and management would be addressed regularly. When people in this school decided what was important to learn, they would consider the variety of opinions and beliefs of people with different styles. According to McCarthy's model, for example, it would be important that curriculum have personal meaning and answer the question "Why?" It also would be important that curriculum develop new knowledge based on accurate information to answer the question "What?"; be practical and deal with reality and personal application so that for each learner it answered the question "How?"; and be innovative, inspiring, and create new possibilities so that it would answer the question "If?"

A curriculum based on this comprehensive definition of learning would look at the content, skills, and attitudes the school wanted students to develop to be sure that all aspects of each area were considered.

By the same token the question of who makes curriculum decisions could also be answered through the 4MAT System. It is important to think about why the decision is being made and therefore to consider who is in the position to answer "Why?" Also important is defining what knowledge is important and recognizing that the varied interests of learners need to be considered. Those who care about the practical applications of learning—those who eventually will employ the students—also need to be involved in the decision. Finally, we must include those who seek a sense of purpose and inspiration from learning. They, too, would need a voice in curriculum decisions. Currently, one only needs to look at a few commercial texts to see that the designers are not representing these different perspectives.

How would curriculum in such a school be organized? If attention to individual differences were a primary concern, it would be clear that constant sequential organization would lead to an emphasis on limited aspects of knowledge and application, appealing to only a few learners. If a larger perspective were included, relationships, meanings, intuition, personal applications, hypothesis testing, observation, understanding, and appreciation would all be included in the organization. Therefore, curriculum could be organized sequentially and also through themes, through the use of webs, and with opportunities for in-depth study. Different organization frameworks would appeal to different learners.

It is clear that the issues surrounding curriculum decisions are extremely complex. When we add to those issues the complexity of human diversity, we can understand why the easy road for many is to let textbook companies and curriculum "experts" make the decisions. But whatever our professional roles, we make curriculum decisions daily. Whether we acknowledge our biases openly or not, we all have some basic assumptions that are reflected in the decisions we make about what's important to learn and how that learning is organized. We need to be aware of our own perspectives, which determine our behavior. When we take up the challenge that understanding human diversity implies, we must continually seek to answer the question: What is appropriate for each individual person in school?

13

Instructional Methods:

Modalities—Barbe and Swassing and Dunn and Dunn

"Everything, men, animals, trees, stars, we are all one substance involved in the same terrible struggle. What struggle? . . . Turning matter into spirit."

Zorba scratched his head (and said,) "I've got a thick skull boss, I don't grasp these things easily. Ah, if only you could dance all that you've just said, then I'd understand. . . . Or if you could tell me all that in a story, boss."

—NIKOS KAZANTZAKIS
—*ZORBA THE GREEK*

Two roads diverged in a wood and I—
I took the one less traveled by,
And that has made all the difference.

—ROBERT FROST
"The Road Not Taken"

Mrs. Chock-Eng is reading this well-known poem to her English class. When she finishes, she encourages the students to discuss what the poem means to them. Some of the children are very eager to share their ideas and experiences. Others, however, are drifting off; they seem distracted and begin to fidget and look at the clock. After a few more minutes, Mrs. Chock-Eng gives the children a homework assignment to memorize the poem. The next day some of the children enthusiastically want to recite the poem, while others are sullen, nervous, or disinterested.

In another school several miles away, Mr. St. George is also using Frost's poem. Before he introduces the poem, he asks for some volunteers to act out a situation where a decision has to be made. After several such short scenarios followed by a brief discussion about making decisions, he passes out paper and crayons and asks the students to draw something about making a choice. He then reads the poem aloud to the class. For a second reading he uses an overhead transparency with the poem written on it and asks the class to follow along. Finally, he asks the students how their skits and drawings might relate to the poem they have just been reading. A lively discussion ensues in which most of the class participates. In a little while he brings the discussion to a close and gives the assignment for the next day. Written on the board, it includes several choices, among which are memorizing the poem, illustrating it with a drawing, or acting out an example of its message. The next day the students return, anxious to share the projects they have chosen to do.

The All-Important *How*

If we analyze the above situation in terms of style, we can see that in the first case the poem was presented in only one way and therefore appealed to a narrow range of students' styles. In the second case, because the poem was approached with a variety of techniques, it appealed to a much wider group of learners. It is likely that the overall objective of the lesson in each case was the same: that the students interpret the message of Robert Frost's poem. The difference in learning that occurs for the students, however, is directly related to *how* the material is presented.

This how, the method and the technique of instruction, can make a tremendous difference in the ultimate success of learning. We have all been in situations where, despite a positive attitude and strong motivation, we found it difficult to learn because of the method used to present the material. But when given a choice of methods, we select one that we know from experience works for us. As we observe people learning to use computers, for example, we notice some use a hands-on approach while others appreciate modeling and demonstration. Some new users purchase how-to books and carefully read them; others sign up for classes to learn with a teacher's direction. We exhibit the same variety when learning physical skills. Some of us learn to ski by getting on the skis and plunging down the slope. Others take lessons, watching carefully as the instructor demonstrates.

It is astonishing to see how improved our understanding can be when something is expressed in a different way. Some of us will say, "Can you show me what you're talking about?" when we want to visualize an idea. We say, "Please tell me what I'm looking at," when we want someone to explain a diagram or picture. Others will plead, "Let me try it myself!" when they want to check understanding. Each situation represents an attempt to understand something in the way that makes most sense to the individual.

Experienced teachers know through common sense and their daily work that children learn in different ways. This obviously leads them to try different techniques and methods. Knowledge of learning styles can make this effort more systematic and more thorough. In this chapter we will discuss the differences in modality strengths and preferences among learners as a basis for describing the importance of variety in instructional techniques and methods.

Differences in Modality Strengths and Preferences

Modalities generally refer to the sensory channels through which we receive and give messages. A number of researchers have identified modality areas as examples of differences in style. Much of Maria Montessori's work was built on an understanding that children need visual, auditory, tactile, and kinesthetic involvement in learning. More recently, different modality preferences and strengths have been identified and studied to help us understand children's and adults' learning styles.

Walter Barbe, Raymond Swassing, and Michael Milone of The Ohio State University focus on the modality differences in their definition of learning styles. "A modality is any of the sensory channels through which an individual receives and retains information. . . . [S]ensation, perception, and memory constitute what we are calling modality" (Barbe and Swassing, 1979/1988, p. 1). Rita and Kenneth Dunn include modality in their comprehensive battery of the elements that affect learning. Their colleague, Marie Carbo (1981), has included the modality area in her assessment of students' reading styles. (See Chapter 11 for more information about their models.) The auditory, visual, and kinesthetic/tactile modalities are identified as the most important sensory channels for education.

Auditory learners use their voices and their ears as the primary mode for learning. They remember what they hear and what they themselves express verbally. When something is hard to understand, they want to talk it through. When they're excited and enthusiastic about learning, they want to verbally express their response. And when an assignment is given orally, they remember it without writing it down. These learners love class discussion, grow by working and talking with others, and appreciate a teacher taking time to explain something to them. They also are distracted easily by sound because they attend to all of the noises around them, but ironically they will interrupt a quiet moment by talking because they find the silence itself disturbing.

When these students read, they vocalize the words, sometimes mumbling, sometimes moving their lips. When they want to remember something, they will say it aloud, sometimes several times, because the oral repetition will implant it in their minds. When they tell you something, they assume you will remember it. They have difficulty when a teacher asks them to work quietly at their desks for an extended period of time, or their parents ask them to study in a quiet room. For some auditory students, their abilities serve them well in learning music, foreign languages, and other areas that depend on good auditory discrimination.

Some learners find their visual modality is much stronger in helping them understand and remember new concepts and skills. They want to actually see words written down, a picture of something being described, a timeline to remember events in history, or the assignment written on the board. These learners will be very attuned to all of the physical things in the classroom and will appreciate a pleasant and orderly environment. They often will organize their own materials carefully and will decorate their work spaces. As young children they want to see the pictures in the storybooks, and when they get older, they seek illustrations, diagrams, and charts to help them understand and remember information. They appreciate being able to follow what a teacher is presenting with material written on an overhead transparency or in a handout. They review and study material by reading over their notes and by recopying and reorganizing in outline form.

Some learners find that they prefer, and actually learn better, when they touch and are physically involved in what they are studying. These learners want to act out a situation, to make a product, to do a project, and to be busy with their learning. As young children, they want to build and handle materials constantly, and this desire stays with them as they choose shop and home economics courses in high school. They find that when they physically do something, they understand it and they remember it. As they get older, many of them take notes to keep their hands busy, but they may never reread the jottings. They learn to use the computer by actually trying it, experimenting, and practicing. They learn concepts in social studies by simulating experiences in the classroom. They become interested in poetry by becoming physically involved in the thoughts expressed. Many of these learners want to be as active as possible during the learning experience. They express their enthusiasm by jumping up and getting excited when something is going well. And when asked to sit still for long periods, they fidget. Thus, they're often labeled hyperactive.

These different preferences and strengths in modality areas are familiar to most educators. We also know that many successful learners can function in more than one modality. The ability to bring a multimodal approach to learning has tremendous payoff throughout the years of schooling. Students with mixed modality strengths have a better chance of success than those with a single modality strength because they can process information in whatever way it is presented.

In addition, many successful students have learned from experience to use their modality strengths to transfer learnings from weaker areas. For example, as an aid to memory, strong visual learners typically will write down something presented in an auditory way, and strong auditory learners study with friends to talk over the material. Unfortunately, many young learners do not yet have this transfer ability. Additionally, every classroom has students with strengths in only one sensory area.

Throughout this discussion, the words "strength" and "preference" have been used together or interchangeably. Some researchers believe that modality sensitivity is a preference, something a person expresses a desire for. Others believe modality channels are strengths, which produce more success when used. This difference between preference and strength is illustrated in the variety of instruments used to assess modality style.

The Dunn, Dunn, and Price Learning Style Inventory, described in Chapter 11, uses self-report questions to measure a student's preference for using one or more modalities. The Swassing-Barbe Modality Index, on the other hand, tests modality strength. A student (from toddler through adult) is asked to use plastic shapes to repeat a given pattern. The patterns are presented sequentially in the oral, visual, and kinesthetic/tactile modalities, and a score representing successful repetition of the pattern is totaled for each modality area. The actual numerical score is less important than the relationship of the three modality subscores. One would expect adults to repeat a higher number of patterns successfully. The relationship among one individual's scores describes the modality profile with its particular strengths or deficits. For example, 47 percent auditory, 28 percent visual, and 27 percent kinesthetic would show strong auditory strength.

Because a number of people have studied the modality area, research on various questions sometimes yields conflicting results. One area of disagreement revolves around the percentage of each modality style in the population as a whole and particularly in school-age populations. Barbe and Milone (1981) find that, "Primary grade children are more auditory than visual, and are least well developed kinesthetically" (p. 378). But Marie Carbo (1982) believes that most young readers approach reading through use of their "tactual/kinesthetic/visual skills—their auditory abilities are usually not well developed until 5th or 6th grade" (p. 43).

Another unresolved question is the relationship of modality perception, discrimination, and memory. Is it possible that a learner may have a very strong auditory memory but rather weak auditory discrimination? These issues and others point out that while, on the surface, the study of modality style may seem relatively straightforward, further inquiry reveals the complexities in this model.

The modality area is one of the best known learning style models among educators. For a number of years, people in special education have responded to modality differences in diagnostic and prescriptive work with students who have learning disabilities. A number of textbook companies acknowledge modality differences by suggesting different ways for teachers to present, review, and evaluate the concepts and skills in their materials. These efforts are generally encouraging, but they can be shallow if more than lip-service is not paid to deep individual differences.

In Style with Instructional Methods

In a school that seriously attends to differences in learning styles, the modality concepts help assure that students have an opportunity to hear, see, and do each time a new concept is presented and reinforced. Teachers carefully evaluate their individual lessons to be sure students with different modality strengths find a way to understand the concepts. "Let me tell you," "Let me show you," and "Let's do it," become standard comments in each classroom. When a child says, "I don't understand," the teacher attempts to explain the material in a different way than it was originally presented.

In a school that uses concepts of learning styles to encourage variety in teaching techniques, each staff member works to expand his or her own repertoire of methods, because, "[W]e teach as we learn best, not as we were taught. [Teachers] tend to project their own modality strengths into their selection of materials, teaching strategies and procedures, and methods of reinforcement" (Barbe and Swassing, 1979/1988, p. 14).

Teachers would examine this tendency to present material according to their own style and would seek to augment the presentation in ways that would meet the needs of a variety of students. The strong auditory teacher, for example, would recognize the tendency to explain new concepts and skills verbally, strive to bring more visual examples to the curriculum, and create more ways for the students to be physically involved in learning.

The strong visual teacher would realize the tendency to emphasize the neat presentation of work and to focus on a visual product such as a worksheet. Such teachers would strive to explain lessons verbally, even repeating what is already written. These teachers would also strive to be patient with students who do not have a natural sense of visual order. The strong kinesthetic teacher would understand that not all children are excited by projects and products and would realize that the desire to have all students involved in their learning must include participation by reading and talking as well as doing.

At the same time, a teacher would focus directly on the needs of the students, especially those who are having a difficult time learning. Instead of just presenting the lesson in the same way louder and slower, teachers can "provide supplemental instruction, either individually or in small groups, that is consistent with the modality strengths of the children involved" (Milone, 1980, p. xiii). By working through the students' strongest learning modality, the teacher can then encourage the students to develop strategies to transfer material from weaker modalities.

Let's look at a spelling program in a classroom as a specific example. A teacher attending to diversity in students' styles would be sure that new spelling words were presented orally, visually, and through action. Students would be encouraged to study the words in ways that took advantage of their own modality strength. Tapes would be available for the auditory learner; written lists for the visual learner; and large markers, flash cards, and letter dice for the kinesthetic learner. When it was time for the test, students could be given a choice in the way they might take the test, or the teacher might vary the method of giving the test from week to week.

The importance of using a variety of teaching methods is certainly not a new idea in education. But understanding differences in style can help strengthen a teacher's commitment to use diverse methods and bring a systematic approach to this effort.

14

Assessment and Evaluation:

Gardner's Multiple Intelligences

I'm inclined to think that being a success is tied up
very closely with being one's own kind of individual.

—ELEANOR ROOSEVELT

Jessica and Miranda have been friends since elementary school. Because of her interest in music, Jessica now attends a large high school on the other side of the city. She and Miranda still see each other frequently in the neighborhood and often compare notes on the differences in their schools.

The girls have just received their first semester report cards. Jessica is frustrated with a B *in her English class. She tells her friend she can't understand how the teacher gave her this grade when she had almost all* A *marks on her quizzes. The rest of the grades were what she expected and she throws the report card on the corner of her desk.*

Miranda is astonished. "Is that all there is?" she says. "Sure, what else would there be?" Jessica responds. "Well, wow, look at my report card," replies Miranda and shows Jessica two pages, with each subject area delineating key concepts and skills in which she has been rated as 'competent' or 'developing.' In addition, there are several lines for teachers' comments, and all of the teachers have written a few phrases. "Boy," Miranda says, "my English teacher really knows me well. Look at this! 'Needs to focus on sequence in writing.' Remember when our 4th grade teacher used to talk about that same thing? I guess I still need to work on it."

"Wow!" Jessica responds, "Your report card is so different. Does all that stuff really make sense?" "Oh yeah!" Miranda answers, "We talk about it a lot in class. Most criteria for work are posted in our classrooms so we know what we are aiming for."

Assessment and evaluation issues have long been of concern to educators, parents, and the general public. Many students place a lot of value on grades, partially as a reflection of the importance and significance given to them by their parents and the public. When newspapers report achievement levels of local school districts, the story is often featured prominently and is read as an indication of the quality of the school system. Yet, as the above scenario exhibits, a numerical score or a letter grade conveys very little information.

Assessment and Evaluation Issues

Assessment and evaluation serve several purposes and cater to several constituencies. Students want to know how they are doing. This means an identification of their competencies, a comment on quality by someone with more expertise, and their standing in comparison to their peers. Some students are sophisticated enough to want to know the stage of development of their particular skills and learnings. They think about mastery and try to figure out how close they are to it. Parents are anxious to learn about their child's progress in relationship to others of a comparable age and background. At the same time, they look for specific information about their child's unique abilities and potential.

Administrative and support staff in the school district look at general trends so they can evaluate success of programs and teaching methods within the schools. The general public, whose taxes support the public school system, is anxious to know if the system is successful as rated by an objective measure. And teachers are intimately involved with assessment and evaluation on a regular basis in order to modify, adjust, and adapt their instruction. When teachers are clear about the expected outcomes of the learnings, regular assessment of students' progress toward these outcomes is an integral part of the instructional process.

Initially, the terms assessment and evaluation were used interchangeably, but they have distinct definitions and purposes. Assessment comes from the Latin *assidere,* meaning to sit beside. In education, assessment is an ongoing process of observing, describing, interpreting, and recording achievement. Assessment is an active, participatory process. Its purpose is to extend learning and to encourage depth, quality, and reflection. By its very definition, it is multidimensional. It should always be directly connected to learning.

Evaluation is more closely linked with objective measurement or judgment about collected information. It is a more summative task with the purpose of identifying a level of success. While an effective evaluation process certainly can foster further learning, this is not often the case in reality. In many situations, evaluation leads to categorization: students who "pass" go forward; students with deficits are referred for help. Seldom are learners actively involved in evaluation.

It is not surprising that evaluation has not responded to individual differences. Its very purpose is often linked to standardization. Assessment, on the other hand, can be sensitive to individual learning differences.

Several issues about evaluation and assessment need to be examined in light of learning styles theories. For example, identification of specific outcomes for assessment and evaluation is an area of frequent discussion and some controversy. Most people agree that students should master basic skills in literacy and computation, but specific content goals touch upon the individual values of families and communities. Attention to the history of cultural minorities and political controversies have different importance in different school districts. Emphasis on bilingual study and attention to environmental issues also vary from community to community.

Should there be national standards? If so, to what level of specificity? Should all 5th graders study the American Revolution? Should there be a list of literature that all students should read? Who should be involved in setting these standards, and how should they be monitored? Can evaluation of the end result be an objective, quantifiable number in which comparisons can be made across classrooms so that students, parents, educators, and other constituencies have a systematic measure of success?

While all of these issues have been addressed in education over the years, the area of assessment has been recently infused with a positive energy as many educators strive to make a direct connection between assessment and the instructional process. Many states are grappling with their role in setting standards and monitoring successes. The differences between assessment and evaluation are regularly articulated. Methods of assessment are examined with the goal of adding more variety and authenticity to measurement of students' performance.

In the classroom, and at district and state levels, educators have proposed a variety of ways to document, measure, and record student learning. Student self-reflection is an essential part of this effort. The active recognition of the connection of assessment with curriculum and instruction is also a part of this recent attention. Because we should not bother assessing something that is unclear or unimportant, we need to regularly examine what's worth learning. The best assessment strategies will point to next steps in the development of learning. Thus, instructional methods are directly connected to assessment procedures.

Perhaps most important, an educator's attitude toward learning and learners is a fundamental part of assessment application. Thus, it is essential to examine classroom conditions necessary for the establishment of an assessment culture. All of these innovations in assessment will benefit from serious attention to students' learning style differences. To consider this connection further, we will examine the work of Howard Gardner and his descriptions of multiple ways of knowing called *multiple intelligences*.

Gardner's Multiple Intelligences

Howard Gardner has had a long-standing interest in studying human potential for learning and the intricacies of the human mind and brain. He is intrigued by how genius, excellence, and competence are exhibited in a variety of ways. A talented musical composer communicating with a listener, for example, exhibits a genius that could genuinely be labeled "intelligence." Gardner also recognizes that much of our view of intelligence is culturally related. What is considered mundane, normal, everyday behavior in one culture might be considered unusual and extraordinary in another. Additionally, cultures that place a high value on certain kinds of behaviors teach their children from the earliest stages the skills to develop these behaviors, and many people within the culture become extraordinarily capable in these areas. For example, a culture that values spacial acuity gives its youth a variety of experiences and vocabulary for developing sophisticated spatial skills.

Gardner articulated his theory in his 1983 book *Frames of Mind*, describing multiple perspectives on intelligence. He took to task the narrow view of Western society's emphasis on linguistic and mathematical intelligence and added and named several more intelligences.

While Gardner continues to explore this area, he initially proposed seven distinct intelligences. Everyone possesses them, but they are generally developed unevenly. It would be more typical for an individual to be highly capable in two or three areas and less capable in the others. In 1997, Gardner added an eighth intelligence, the naturalist (in Checkley, 1997). The eight intelligences are:

• *Linguistic intelligence,* in which a person is facile with language and words. This person generally has a highly developed vocabulary, an ability to communicate in a clear and interesting way orally or in writing, and a sophisticated receptivity to language.

• *Logical-mathematical intelligence,* in which a person is especially competent in discerning quantitative relationships and connections, particularly related to calculations and scientific areas. This person is skilled in recognizing and developing logical systems.

• *Spatial intelligence,* in which a person skillfully manipulates images, recognizes, and creates visual forms mentally as well as on paper, and in designs of various kinds.

• *Bodily kinesthetic intelligence,* in which a person has graceful body movements and an awareness of his or her own and others' positions in space. This person has a physical agility that is often illustrated by an extraordinary ability in particular physical areas.

• *Musical intelligence,* in which a person exhibits acute sensitivity to sound and an ability to create and communicate through tones and rhythmic patterns.

- *Interpersonal intelligence,* in which a person perceptively understands the perspective of another person, relates to others easily, and is skilled at working cooperatively.

- *Intrapersonal intelligence,* in which a person reflects on himself or herself thoughtfully, is perceptive about personal abilities, and attuned to personal history.

- *Naturalist intelligence,* in which a person is interested in and knowledgeable about the natural world and effectively discriminates among sensory things.

In the years since the theory of multiple intelligences was presented, a number of educational applications have been made. The theory of multiple intelligences rang true for many educators. They recognized their past and current students as examples of people with diverse profiles of intelligence. Educators have embraced this theory with enthusiasm, and a number of books about educational applications, including Gardner's 1991 book *The Unschooled Mind,* explicitly discuss the connection between education and the multiple intelligences theories.

Thomas Armstrong's (1987) book *In Their Own Way* was written for parents to help them deepen their understanding of their child's uniqueness. He introduces the seven intelligences to help parents support their own children's intelligence strengths at home and in school. In 1994, he published *Multiple Intelligences in the Classroom* to expand his ideas. Recently, he has written about the proliferation of learning disability diagnosis especially ADD and ADHD. His 1995 book, *The Myth of the ADD Child,* argues that students' learning styles and various intelligences need to be examined before a disability is assumed and medication prescribed.

David Lazear also published several books focused on the practical applications of multiple intelligences. His 1994 book, *Multiple Intelligences Approaches to Assessment,* gives a variety of examples of assessment strategies. Bruce and Linda Campbell have written about classroom activities that accommodate the initial seven intelligences. Their books, *Teaching and Learning Through Multiple Intelligences* and *The Multiple Intelligences Handbook,* describe a variety of strategies teachers can use to present content in seven ways corresponding to the intelligence areas (Campbell, Campbell, & Dickinson, 1996; Campbell, 1994). Finally, Robin Fogarty and Judy Stoehr (1994) address thematic teaching in *Integrating Curricula with Multiple Intelligences*. Each of these resources offers teachers practical ideas for using the theory of multiple intelligences in the classroom. While structured classroom activities are clearly valuable, Gardner (1995) is cautious about quick-fix applications.

> Note that it is reasonable, for certain purposes, to indicate that a child seems to have a relative strength in one intelligence and a relative weakness in another. However, these descriptions should be mobilized in order to help students perform better in meaningful activities and perhaps even to show that a label was premature or erroneous. (p. 207)

A number of schools have restructured their curriculum and instruction to explicitly accommodate the various intelligences. In many classrooms around the country, teachers have made overt efforts to respond to students' different intelligences. Some of these applications are instructionally based so that teachers regularly apply musical, kinesthetic, artistic, and group-process strategies to help students learn particular concepts and content. In some classrooms, students are taught about the theory of multiple intelligences and encouraged to reflect upon their current strengths to work to develop these skills and stretch into other areas.

The theory of multiple intelligences challenges us to look at the content we currently teach and to broaden the aspects of the content students study. A student who is highly intelligent in a musical area, for example, will be interested in the rhythm of a poem more than analyzing the linguistic vocabulary. A student who is highly intelligent in a bodily kinesthetic way will be interested in finding physical ways to show the action of the poem. The highly interpersonal student will want to discuss the relationships of the ideas in the poem to people's current values and lives.

In a 1997 interview, Gardner commented on implementation of multiple intelligences.

> Although there is no single MI route, it's very important that a teacher take individual differences among kids very seriously.

You cannot be a good MI teacher if you don't want to know each child and try to gear how you reach and how you evaluate to that particular child. The bottom line is a deep interest in children and how their minds are different from one another, and in helping them use their minds well. (In Checkley, 1997, p. 11)

Multiple Intelligences and Assessment and Evaluation

Early in *Frames of Mind*, Gardner (1983) wrote: "Only if we expand and reformulate our view of what counts as human intellect will we be able to devise more appropriate ways of assessing it and more effective ways of educating it" (p. 4). Here he refers to assessing intelligence, but the same statement can be applied to assessment of various competencies. Indeed, he later wrote in *The Unschooled Mind*: "Students learn in ways that are identifiably distinctive. The broad spectrum of students—and perhaps the society as a whole—would be better served if disciplines could be presented in a number of ways and learning could be assessed through a variety of means" (1991, p. 12).

It seems obvious that diversity in ways of learning would demand variety in ways of assessing and evaluating learning. With a broader definition of what we want students to know, the assessment of their success attaining the knowledge will also be broader. Does a student have to demonstrate an understanding of a poem only through verbal expression, or could students show their understanding in ways that might take advantage of their extraordinary intelligence in another area such as visual, spatial, interpersonal, or musical?

We all have had the experience of understanding something but not being able to find an appropriate way to express that understanding. Students will often say, "Let me show you! I can't explain it, but I can show it to you." Another student may say, "I can't find the words to tell you, but I can do it." Another student may say, "I can't analyze it on paper, but I can tell you where it fits in my life." Developing assessments responsive to these types of statements are as valuable as the linguistic and quantifiable assessments that are common in most schools.

Attention to multiple intelligences will help educators intentionally design diverse ways for students to express their mastery of knowledge and the quality of their learning. To have three choices for showing your knowledge, all of which require linguistic intelligence, is less choice than three options that allow different expressions of intelligence. For example, three different essay topics would be much less of a choice than an essay as one choice, the composition of a rap song or a ballad as another, and the design of a poster as the third.

In a 1997 article, Harvey Silver, Richard Strong, and Matthew Perini describe ways to assess learning that represent different intelligences and acknowledge various learning styles. For example, a personal linguistic learner might write a letter or conduct an interview to demonstrate learning. A more analytic linguistic learner might defend a decision and interpret a text to demonstrate the same learning. With the guidance of multiple intelligences and learning styles descriptions, teachers can intentionally design legitimately different ways to assess mastery and competence.

Additionally, learning style and intelligence differences can help teachers broaden the expectations of the content learned. In the poetry example above, one student may be very interested in the words, another in the rhyme, and a third in the emotional meaning of the poem. Each of these areas are important and valuable perspectives on the poem. If only one is emphasized, some students are denied a way to understand the poem. In the study of history, stories can be emphasized along with facts. In mathematics, patterns are as important as computation. Many teachers currently address various aspects of the content they teach. A study of multiple intelligences and learning styles helps them to expand this work and be more intentional about the application.

The assessment and evaluation areas are among the more important areas in education because decisions involving them have a broad impact. Attention to diversity among learners is essential for assessment to be genuine and to be helpful to each student's progress. And attention to diversity among the school population is essential for any evaluation of the school's success to be meaningful.

Part III

Responding to Diversity

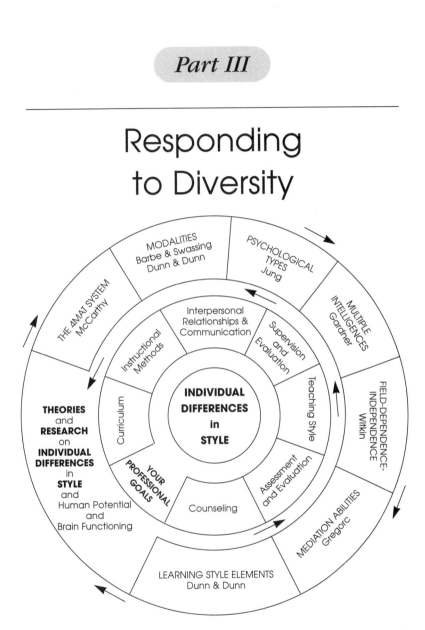

Making use of style concepts implies clarifying one's own beliefs about individual differences and identifying professional goals. Application then requires knowledge of theories and research on individual differences (personal style, human potential, and brain functioning). As the wheel is rotated, beliefs, goals, and theories and research are brought together to guide implementation.

15

Common Questions and Issues

I desire that there be as many different persons in the world as possible; I would have each one be very careful to find out and preserve his own way.

—HENRY DAVID THOREAU

Because the study of style is so varied and complex, a number of questions and unresolved issues often arise. This chapter highlights some of the more important questions in learning styles research concerning origin, development, and change; gender; neutrality, intelligence, and achievement; assessment; and choosing a model.

Origin, Development, and Change

What forms our basic personality style? The answer seems to be that both nature and nurture play a part in the origin of style. Psychologists especially believe that we are born with the foundation of our style patterns. Carl Jung (in Wickes, 1927/1966) considered origin of type when he discussed the unique personalities of each child in a family.

> For all lovers of theory, the essential fact . . . is that the things which have the most powerful effect upon children do not come from the conscious state of the parents but from their unconscious background. . . . Here as elsewhere in practical psychology we are constantly coming up against the experience

that in a family of several children only one of them will react to the unconscious of the parents with a marked degree of identity, while the others show no such reaction. The specific constitution of the individual plays a part here that is practically decisive. (pp. xix–xx)

Psychologist Frances Wickes (1927/1966), working under Jung's guidance, wrote that, "We must think of life as developing from within as well as from without. . . [;] each [child] bears within himself the germ of his own individuality" (pp. 13–14). Recent researchers, such as Barbe and Swassing (1979), also recognize both nature and nurture: "The definition we are proposing acknowledges the role of both heredity and the environment in shaping an individual's modality strengths" (p. 5).

Certainly, experience plays an important part in who we are. One way to think about the balance of nature and nurture is to consider the aspects of a person that style describes. We have related style to differences in cognition, conceptualization, affect, and behavior. Certain of these traits are probably more affected by experience than others. One could argue that cognitive and conceptual characteristics are deep-rooted in a person's internal world, but affect and behavior are shaped by external experience. As we consider different researchers' explanations for the roots of style, their reasoning often reflects their basic definition of style. Those who focus primarily on behavior are likely to attribute more importance to experience, for example.

A number of researchers discuss the importance of the development of style. Their message is that both competence and self-esteem come from successfully using natural style traits. If I'm naturally inclined toward certain patterns of behavior, I will be at my best in these areas. If I am praised for these behaviors, I will feel good about myself. If my natural traits are not valued, they will not develop to their fullest, and I may wonder, "What's wrong with me?" One mother illustrated this dilemma in a parents' workshop when she shared a story about her son.

Let me tell you about my son. He's always daydreaming, staring into space. It really worries me that he does nothing. Today,

136

for example, he was staring out the window, so I timed him. Ten minutes! Then he turned to me and he said, "Mom, the moon is banana shaped." Then he turned toward the window again; four more minutes. "Mom, if the moon is banana shaped, it can't be round." Do you see what I mean? Why would he waste his time just looking out the window at the moon?

This mother went on to explain that while she values action, learning about style helped her realize that her child obviously places a value on imagining. She now realizes that to develop his own style fully, this child will need to feel accepted and loved for what he does naturally and easily. If he feels this acceptance, he eventually will be more receptive to his mother's emphasis on action, because a positive self-esteem opens us to growth and change. In the ideal situation, this child could learn to value and use his strengths and develop skills to approach life in other ways. But if his mother does not value his dreaming, the child may come to question his own strengths.

Understanding the importance of nature as one root of personality and style guides many interactions. If we believe that people can change easily, we are more likely to demand change. For a teacher, this is a daily decision. Does a teacher accept a child's fundamental way of behaving and work with that for growth? Or does a teacher strive for uniform behaviors and expect every child to attain them easily?

One workshop participant shared that learning about style brought to mind planting the flower seeds from a "mixed bloom" package. You must prepare your garden and tend to the early plants to get the full benefit of the blooms, but you can't change the type of flower the seeds will produce. In the same way, a parent is responsible for tending a child, but the child will blossom as his or her own individual.

A final issue with nature and nurture is that of helping a person to learn behaviors that are not "natural." We often minimize the value of things that come easy and focus more on those that are less comfortable. We tell an introverted child to be more outgoing, an extravert to learn self-control, a concrete sequential to loosen up. Certainly, these are valid goals for developing social and learning flexibility. Yet a young person often hears, "Okay, you're good at this, but put that

aside and work on this other thing." Children don't get the full benefit of becoming secure with their natural strengths. Well-meaning
efforts to strengthen undeveloped behaviors can actually damage a
fragile self-esteem. Early development of style strengths leads to self-
confidence and the ability to stretch and take risks later in life.

Can we change our style? In a review of the Myers-Briggs research, Hoffman and Betkouski (1981) conclude that "patterns of behavior are deep in each person's psychological makeup. Lawrence's
model refers to this behavior as being as unchangeable as the stripes
on a tiger. . . . Keirsey said it another way, 'The unfolding rose may
blossom to its fullest but will never be a sunflower'" (p. 25).

In response to the same question, Claudia Cornett (1983) says,
"[W]hile the learning style blueprint is initially based on inheritance
and prenatal influences, a person's learning predisposition is subject
to qualitative changes resulting from maturation and environmental
stimuli. . . . *Throughout life, all people are subject to changes within
a relatively stable overall style structure*" (p. 12, our italics).

As mature adults, we "change" our behaviors to respond to the
demands of particular situations, but do we really change the core of
our person? Because educators recognize that certain style traits are
related to success in specific school tasks, the question of changing
styles is very important. When a learner's style is dysfunctional for
specific school tasks, who adapts: the learner or the school? This
question brings mixed responses from researchers, based to some
extent on their beliefs about the feasibility of changing style.

As we discussed earlier in this book, we believe it is most realistic
to talk about development of specific skills to respond to the demands
of school and society. When this development is done in a manner that
honors natural style strengths, students can gain desired skills. A global
learner can be taught to organize ideas with a mind map, browse a
book chapter before reading to get the whole picture, and then read
carefully for specific items. Auditory learners can be encouraged to
"say" ideas in their own heads before blurting out responses.

Gender

Is an individual's style related to gender? Researchers who have
examined this question generally find that socialization plays a role

in the development of style differences in both sexes. For example, the Myers-Briggs research (Lawrence, 1979/1982/1993) found that women are more likely to be on the feeling end of the thinking/feeling continuum while men tend to be close to the thinking end, with a 60 percent to 40 percent differentiation.

However, because we know that women are generally expected to behave with more feeling types of characteristics and thus are reinforced for those behaviors, it is not surprising to find this difference. Another commonly held social stereotype, that boys are more kinesthetic than girls, was not substantiated, however, in Barbe's modality research (Barbe & Milone, 1982). For now, we must conclude that research currently does not offer substantial evidence that style is innately different for each sex.

Neutrality, Intelligence, and Achievement

Some ask, "Is there a 'best' style?" Throughout this book, we've defined style as neutral. This implies that there is no better, best, good, or poor style. Most researchers discuss the potential positives and negatives of various patterns of style. For example, Witkin and Goodenough observe that

> . . . the field-dependence-independence dimension is bipolar with regard to level, in the sense that it does not have clear "high" and "low" ends. Its bipolarity makes the dimension value neutral, in the sense that each pole has qualities that are adaptive in particular circumstances. . . . We thus see that field dependence and field independence are not inherently "good" or "bad." (1981, p. 59)

This fundamental notion is the basis of valuing diversity. Viewing every style as having inherent qualities that can be potential strengths eliminates the temptation to judge a person's style solely against set criteria.

But are people with a certain style "smarter"? A number of researchers have studied the relationship between style and intelligence. They have found that some tasks on intelligence tests actually measure style. Barbe and Swassing (1979) believe that Binet and Simon's original measurements, which deal with "memorizing series of digits and matching patterns of beads, were primarily tests of modality strengths" (p. 33). Also, the Wechsler Block Design, Object Assembly, and Picture Completion subtests, all of which require restructuring, have been shown to favor a field-independent style (Witkin & Goodenough, 1981, p. 61).

After acknowledging the testing bias, however, the majority of style researchers agree with Hoffman and Betkouski (1981), who concluded after a comprehensive review of type research that intelligence is independent from style: "Type theory indicates . . . differences are related to varying interests and not necessarily a superiority of ability of one type over another" (p. 18).

On the other hand, a number of research studies have found correlation between style and achievement in school. It does seem that students benefit from having certain style characteristics that lead to more consistent success with school tasks. As early as 1927, Jungian child psychologist Wickes reported:

> Usually it is the thinking type of child who shows to best advantage in the school, for school is primarily the place of intellectual development, and thinking is the intellectual form of adaptation to reality. (1927/1966, p. 120)

In 1997, McCarthy reported the same bias: "*Unfortunately, schools tend to honor only one aspect of perceiving—thinking*" (1997, p. 49, italics in original).

Reviews of the type literature also have shown that "intuitives appear to have the greater potential for success in school from the beginning. Most classroom instruction is based on the use of symbols, an area in which intuitives show up well" (Hoffman & Betkouski, 1981, p. 18). This particular dichotomy between dominant sensing and intuitive type students was dramatically illustrated in an extensive research study in Florida conducted by the Governor's Task Force on Disruptive Youth. A sample of more than 500 adults who did not complete 8th grade showed that 99.6 percent were sensing types. The same study showed that of 671 finalists for National Merit Scholarships, 83 percent were intuitives (McCaulley & Natter, 1974/1980, p. 128).

This is a dilemma. If style is not directly related to intelligence, why are some styles more successful in school? Another aspect of this question is evidence that people of all styles can be successful in professions, business, and industry, and this success is a matter of the right style match to the requirements of a particular profession or job.

It has been interesting to note, for example, that in the past two decades, studies of industry productivity emphasize the importance of people skills and intuition, which have not been visibly valued in Western industrialized societies. In their description of successful American companies, *In Search of Excellence* authors Peters and Waterman (1982) focus on the importance of these approaches and patterns.

> [W]e have to stop overdoing things on the rational side. . . . Our imaginative, symbolic right brain is at least as important as our rational, deductive left. We reason by stories at least as often as with good data. "Does it feel right?" counts for more than "Does it add up?" or "Can I prove it?" (pp. 54–55)

In schools, too, we need to continue to examine which qualities are emphasized and valued. Are we giving all styles equal chances for success? Because research and experience confirm the value of all styles, we should teach students by example that each person has the potential for success and satisfaction in school and beyond—whatever his or her style may be.

Assessment of Style

How do we know what a person's style is? When should we assess style? Who should assess style? How valid are assessment instruments?

There are basically five ways to assess style (see Figure 15.1). The first is through self-report instruments. This is the most common assessment technique commercially available and includes the Gregorc Style Delineator, the Dunns' Learning Style Inventory (LSI), and the Myers-Briggs Type Indicator (MBTI). These and similar instruments are available for use in education, business, and other professions. These instruments ask a person to rank responses to some questions and/or words, often forcing a choice. They are scored to show the person's style through the patterns of the responses.

FIGURE 15.1

WAYS TO ASSESS STYLE*

INVENTORIES

Direct self-report:
- Learning Styles Inventory (LSI) (Dunn, Dunn, & Price)
- Myers-Briggs Type Indicator (MBTI) (Myers-Briggs)
- Communicating Styles Survey (Mok)

Indirect self-report:
- Gregorc Style Delineator (Gregorc)
- Learning Style Inventory (Kolb, used by McCarthy)

TESTS
- Embedded Figures Test (Witkin)
- Swassing-Barbe Modality Index (Barbe & Swassing)

INTERVIEW
- Open-ended conversation
- With "inventory" questions
- Writing one's own profile as a learner

OBSERVATION
- Checklists (Lawrence, Barbe, & Swassing)
- Anecdotal records

ANALYSIS OF PRODUCTS OF LEARNING
- Achievements
- Errors (e.g., reading miscue-analysis)

*All instruments cited are listed in the References.

With self-report instruments, people give direct information about themselves and often feel very comfortable with the results. These instruments have a potential weakness, however, in that people's responses may reflect wishful thinking and mood rather than reality. Perhaps more important, as Jung (1921/1971) notes: "In respect of one's own personality, one's judgment is as a rule extraordinarily clouded" (p. 3).

The second way to assess style is a test of a particular skill or task. The Embedded Figures Test described in Chapter 9 and the Swassing-Barbe Modality Index described in Chapter 13 are examples of this type of instrument. In a test assessment, a specific task has been shown to correlate with style characteristics, and the degree of success with the task indicates the style. A test assessment has the advantage of being objective, but it is limited to measurement of skill in a specific task, and extensions are inferred.

The third way to assess style is to ask a person directly. An interview may use questions from a self-report instrument or may be open ended. With an interview, we must be aware that both the interviewer and interviewee are affected by their own styles, so they will both bring their own perspectives to the conversation.

The fourth way to assess style is to observe a person at a task or in a particular situation. A number of researchers encourage teachers to observe students and have provided checklists to help systematize the process (Lawrence, 1979/1982/1993; Barbe & Swassing, 1979). As with an interview assessment, the observation of another person will be colored by the observer's perception, and this interaction needs to be considered.

The fifth method of assessment is to look at the outcomes of a person's behavior. Tasks that are easy and consistently successful for an individual will indicate that person's pattern and approach. By the same token, the activities and situations that are consistently difficult give us information, too. Readers who retain accurate, detailed information but have a difficult time with inferences are indicating something about their style. One teacher we worked with used a miscue-analysis approach to assess the reading style of several students. Identifying patterns in the students' reading errors illustrated their ways of thinking. The results were very dramatic and correlated strongly with several characteristics of style.

The authors of style-discerning instruments point out that no instrument is 100 percent valid for every person. Therefore they suggest diagnosis of styles through the use of more than one technique. The authors of many self-report instruments, for example, encourage people to use interviews and observations in conjunction with their instruments.

When should we assess style? This question must be answered by identifying the purpose of a formal assessment. When teachers assess their own style, they study their own patterns to understand their approaches to teaching. A personal and careful assessment of the style of a learner who is at risk of failing could yield very valuable and helpful information.

But in the case of teachers responsible for large numbers of students, the assessment of each student's style implies having plans to accommodate the individual differences identified. Administrators and teachers in this instance must be clear about the purpose of such an effort. Caution should be exercised in the widespread assessment of style to avoid unrealistic expectations and frustrations.

One example of an appropriate schoolwide assessment comes from a high school that assessed the style of each entering high school freshman. Results were shared with students and entered in their files. Teachers, parents, and students all received general information about style. When they asked specific questions or expressed concerns, the style information was available and applied. Teachers, parents, and students came to see the information as a resource, not an individual evaluation or a mandate for widespread change.

Who should assess style? Although many of the instruments and tests can be administered without formal training, it would be naive to assume that anyone administering an instrument would be able to effectively use its results. Educators need a depth and breadth of knowledge about style when they assess individuals or groups. Too often, the first thing a person wants to do after an initial introduction to style is administer an assessment to others. Although this may provide interesting information, it doesn't always serve the ultimate purpose of respecting and responding to individual differences. If that purpose is not served, the assessment bears more relation to determining a person's Zodiac sign than to providing useful data.

Assessment is often thought to be a necessary first step in application of concepts of style, but as we have illustrated previously, many accommodations to style can be made by a genuine acceptance of diversity without specifically labeling the diversity of each person. Consciously accommodating style through variety in curriculum and instructional methods is one such application, which is ultimately beneficial for many learners.

We also need to be aware that however well-validated, each assessment instrument is only as reliable as the purpose it is designed to serve. Assessments of cognitive processing infer behavior; personality instruments make generalizations about approaches to learning; behavior assessments are situational. Because researchers focus their work on certain aspects of personality, and real people are multidimensional, it will not be surprising that any instrument will only give a partial picture.

Assessing style should be approached cautiously and with a clear purpose. The more one understands the many dimensions of style, the less hasty one is to make judgments and impose labels. Appropriate use of style assessment should expand our knowledge of and respect for individual differences.

Choosing a Model

We are frequently asked how one should decide which learning style model to apply. Because we view styles as an approach to the use of methods and consciously do not advocate one model over another, this is not an easy question to answer. For application, it is important to choose a model that fits both the situation and the skills of the person making the application.

In consulting with teachers and administrators in the United States, Canada, and Mexico, we found as much diversity in preference for a model as we did differences within any particular model itself. Some educators adamantly prefer the Myers-Briggs model for its wide application and extensive research base; others favor the McCarthy model or the Dunns' model for the clear, organized, and practical application. Others prefer the work of Anthony Gregorc and successfully use the curriculum applications of Kathleen Butler. Many teachers feel comfortable with Gardner's description of multiple intelligences and implement this model in their classrooms.

This choice is not as difficult as it may sound. For example, if understanding Myers-Briggs comes easy and the applications automatically grow out a level of comfort with that research, then a teacher probably has the best chance of successfully using that model. If, on the other hand, a teacher finds the categories confusing, he or she would probably be best served to continue reading and researching other models until a level of comfort and enthusiasm is achieved. In other words, we advocate that readers trust their professional judgment in making a choice and not rely on the current fad to inform them of which is "best." To facilitate this process, initial training should concentrate on basic concepts and practical applications of learning styles where teachers use the models as examples until they can effectively choose which they are most comfortable with.

We advise educators to learn about more than one specific approach to style. If teachers study only one model, there is a tendency to try to "fit" everyone to the model. With attention to two or three ways of defining style, specific labels can be applied when they fit the situation or person. One child in a class might be a very extreme auditory learner, while another child is an extreme intuitive—labels from different models. At the same time, it is not necessary for practitioners to be knowledgeable about all the research on style. Attention to too many labels and models will lead to frustration and inaction. Some models of style, such as the approaches based on the work of Jung, Gregorc, and McCarthy, have similar descriptions of four personal types based on bipolar dichotomies. Therefore, one of these models and one other choice gives educators a good foundation for application.

To be successful with a specific model, educators must read about and research the model in depth. Application of learning style principles takes time—perhaps as long as five years—to see tangible results in student outcomes and behaviors. Style is not a "quick fix." Reaching individual students requires careful reflection, patience, and care—challenging tasks in an education system that is always looking for the next best thing.

Additionally, when teachers are ready to apply a model, their own style plays a role. Some study theory carefully; others gain deeper understanding through application. Some people jump right into total application following a structured format; others begin with a limited application and build from there.

These three principles—research, application, and commitment—are keys to achieving success in style application. But this still does not provide a specific answer to the question: Which model should an educator choose? Here we are consciously respectful of individual differences. As noted elsewhere in this book, there is no "best" style model, but there is a good choice of a style model for each teacher, classroom, and school situation. The choice must rely on the professional judgment of the teachers, informed by their own style, their own professional experience, and their students' needs.

Finally, it is tempting to try to put the research together to develop a comprehensive, synergistic model. With the development of style theories, both agreement and diversity emerged among the definitions, concepts, applications, and instrumentation. Each researcher creates a personal definition and uses specific vocabulary. Research on styles appears to be in what Kuhn (1961/1970) calls the pre-paradigm period, a time in the research that "is regularly marked by frequent and deep debates over legitimate methods, problems, and standards of solution, though these serve rather to define schools than to produce agreement" (pp. 47–48). This stage is further "characterized by continual competition between a number of distinct views" (p. 4).

A desire for the "best" model of styles can lead educators to look for a program to standardize and synchronize education. But it is a contradiction to believe that any one style theory or instrument will be applicable to each individual. The many models of style instead provide a wealth of resources for schools. It is the educator's job to decide which theory will provide the needed approach for each particular circumstance. This decision does not lead to choosing one "right" definition or model of styles but a thoughtful, comprehensive approach. The genuine acceptance of individual differences is more important than the application of a specific model.

16

Style in Context

A personal sympathy is a great thing in a teacher.
It does its best work, however, when it is in sympathy with the mental movements of others.

—JOHN DEWEY

When learning styles first flourished among educators in the late 1970s, Anthony Gregorc talked about an inevitable revolution if schools took the concept of individual style differences seriously. Current brain researchers echo the same possibility. Though it seems obvious that educators must keep individual differences in the forefront of all decision making, this concept often is ignored in daily practice.

We have seen teachers work together to apply learning styles to instruction—then ignore individual differences when setting discipline policies for the building. Administrators support learning style applications in the classroom, but they often evaluate teachers uniformly, ignoring their individual teaching styles. It is a challenge to apply an *attitude* that honors individuality to all aspects of education. Yet every decision should be approached with the perspective of its impact on a diverse population and in all areas of education. When this attitude and approach becomes ingrained in our thinking, "Learning Styles" will no longer be capitalized. Instead, with lowercase lettering, it will be a regular part of our vocabulary applied to all aspects of education.

Special-Needs Students

Success in traditional classrooms generally requires students to learn what *not* to do: talk, fidget, tap, eat, or move around. Yet evidence shows that some students prefer to learn while talking, fidgeting, tapping, eating, and moving. They are not acting out of a lack of personal discipline but are responding to signals from their central nervous systems. The field of neurophysiology postulates that some students who initially do not succeed in schools fail because their physiological needs are being controverted. (See Garger, 1990, for a full discussion of style and neurophysiology.)

In the larger framework of education, this raises an intriguing question: If a student has trouble learning, is there a learning disability or is the student's style mismatched to the learning situation? A student's needs for mobility, tactile stimulation, intake, kinesthetic learning, and sound in the environment may indicate his or her body's attempt to use adaptive strategies in response to signals from the neural system, which may make focusing on a certain task possible. For example, many students report that silence in the learning environment is distracting. But others report that noise in the environment is distracting. One group cannot learn in the presence of sound—and another group can't learn without it!

We also have seen many examples of cognitive mismatches, such as the predominant use of phonic strategies to teach reading. When holistic, global, and field-dependent learners ask for help, they often are told to decode each word. This approach is antithetical to their style, which focuses on the whole. When they are told to decode each word, these students are pushed further into the problem. The "problem" then becomes even larger—and the students less successful. A disability label is a natural next step. The dependence on one strategy (decoding) to learn a skill (reading) has left many potentially successful learners labeled as "special needs." The same situation exists when active learners are told to learn self-control, then kept from recess as a consequence of their activity in class.

Helping students who exhibit learning problems requires educators to consider any and all of the methodologies they know, especially the research on what style tells us about the individual ways people learn. Research on style and how the neurosystem operates should lead educators to consider natural and less invasive strategies by accommodating style needs before they take more drastic actions like labeling students or prescribing medication.

Parent Education

Parents are perhaps the most important people who need to understand the concept of individual style. The ability to accept the unique personality of each child is tied to understanding style differences. We assume all parents want the best for their children, but "best" should be appropriate for each child in light of his or her natural approaches and personality. Parents may readily accept this concept intellectually but find it difficult to put it into practice.

Because a child's self-esteem is directly tied to approval by parents, especially in the early years, an understanding of style differences can have far-reaching implications later in life. Parents who understand the style patterns of each child as he or she matures will be more successful in helping that child to manage school relationships and tasks and eventually make wise career decisions.

Critical Thinking

Our information-oriented society and the fast pace of technological changes have renewed interest in high-level thinking. Responsible educators recognize that educated people are good thinkers with the ability to analyze, synthesize, apply, and judge the value of their learning.

When we study the processes involved in good thinking, we see that natural perceptions and conceptual processes have a tremendous effect on the way people think. It is easy for some people to use personal reflection, values, and judgments in processing objective information. Some people naturally see the practical application of certain content. And some people readily analyze cause-and-effect relationships. But depending on our mind processes, certain styles of thinking are easy or difficult for different people. Kathleen Butler's work on Style Differentiated Instruction, described in Chapter 10, is one way to carefully consider style differences in developing thinking skills. This challenging area needs to be explored and applied in more depth.

Technology

Computers and their associated technology can revolutionize the way we teach and learn and offer tremendous potential for learning. Here, too, the concepts of style must be considered. People approach technology with different means, different strengths, and certainly different interests. They will find a variety of uses for technology depending on their own needs, experiences, and, of course, styles.

Also important is the way technology offers more options for how to learn, thus accommodating learning style differences. It is possible that a computer program designed for practicing division of fractions, for example, could offer a variety of approaches to learning that concept. A student could select a certain approach, or the computer itself could make the selection based on the kinds of errors, problems, and questions that the student demonstrates with the initial presentation of the concept. Again, technology and learning styles is an important area for further study.

Meaningful Curriculum

A student's motivation to learn is directly related to style of the learning experience as well as the value of the content. The two cannot be separated. A meaningful, intelligent curriculum offers a way for learners to develop understanding by actively creating their own connections to the material.

With the current focus on constructivism, curriculum is organized around broad questions and conceptual problems. Brooks and Brooks (1993) note:

> Structuring curriculum around "big ideas" and broad concepts provides multiple entry points for students: some become engaged through practical responses to problems, some analyze tasks based on models and principles, and others interpret ideas through metaphors and analogies from their unique perspectives. The environment and the use of broad concepts invite each student to participate irrespective of individual styles, temperaments, and dispositions. (p. 58)

Multicultural Goals

While we have stated that the relationship of culture and style is complex, the concepts of style have definite implications for multicultural goals in education. The active recognition of personal differences in style demands an effort to fully understand each individual. This focus extends to an understanding of each person's cultural roots and values. The acceptance of style and cultural values as fundamental strengths of each individual contributes to the development of self-esteem. When we direct our thinking toward a celebration of diversity, we value the cultural uniqueness of each person.

Another goal of multicultural education is respect for differences among people. The study of style can contribute directly to this goal by emphasizing the unique strengths of each person. As we seek to help every student and staff member recognize that it is the very differences among people that bring strength to our educational institutions, this recognition will carry over to attitudes toward society. The goals of multicultural education and style go hand in hand. It would be exciting to see these areas explored together in future studies and applications.

Next Steps

These few examples illustrate the pervasive applications of style concepts. There are many more. Character and moral education is about individual respect. Cooperative learning can be structured to honor individual learning and teaching styles. In all of these areas, we need to acknowledge that people are unique, different from one another in their ways of perceiving, thinking, feeling, and behaving. This fact has the potential to help us avoid fads and nurture the individual in all aspects of education.

17

Accommodating Style

Cherish forever what makes you unique, 'cuz
you're really a yawn if it goes!

—Bette Midler

How should we accommodate differences in style? Must schools and other institutions adapt to the diverse styles of the people who work and study there, or must the people who come to an institution meet its demands? In an individual teaching and learning situation, does the teacher adapt to the student, or the student to the teacher? Do parents adapt to the styles of each child, or do the children adapt to the parents' styles?

One could argue that with the large numbers of people who learn and work in schools, uniform approaches are justified. But when we choose a uniform curriculum program, we definitely decide that students must adapt their styles to the demands of a particular approach. When we require all teachers be evaluated in the same way, we demand that they fulfill the style requirements of that specific evaluation process.

Style researchers have different opinions about this issue. Most believe that schools and teachers must make major adaptations. Some believe that learners must adapt their ways of learning to meet the requirements for success in school, and a few advocate a little bit of each. The Dunns (1975a), for example, urge us to meet the needs of individual learners as often and as frequently as possible. Gregorc (1982a) and Witkin and colleagues (1977) encourage a direct accommodation of style at various times and a conscious mismatch at others to help learners stretch themselves.

McCarthy's 4MAT system is designed to allow part of the instruction to match the learners' strengths and part to intentionally stretch the learner to work with other style approaches. Acknowledging that each student has a dominant learning style pattern, she writes: "But to learn successfully, a student also needs expertise in other learning styles; together these styles form a 'natural cycle of learning'" (1997, p. 46).

We have argued throughout this book that knowing that all people in education have varied styles means that programs, structures, and expectations must respond to that diversity. It is not as important to know the exact style of each person we interact with as it is to act upon the assumption that groups represent a diversity of styles. Therefore, it is important to have variety in all decisions, organizational structures, interactions, and instructional methods.

Although using variety in teaching methods is certainly not a new idea, most educators would agree that we have a long way to go to adequately provide for diversity in learners' styles. Seldom is there only one way to learn. It is this understanding that should encourage us to value various styles in our particular roles in education. Teachers and administrators who understand these concepts consciously attempt to respond to the diversity they regularly encounter in schools.

Practical Strategies

Practical implementation of learning styles concepts and research challenges us to develop two things: understanding of individuality and a commitment to help each individual do his or her best in the learning and teaching process.

Developing Awareness

The very first practical application is awareness of style differences. Do not minimize the importance of awareness. Jumping to action without a deep understanding ultimately leads to weak results or a lack of follow through. To genuinely accommodate individual differences in education takes a serious commitment and a great deal of time, energy, and effort. Before that can happen, it is paramount to understand diversity. Too often, educators apologize for "only" being aware of differences, but an understanding of individual differences leads to subtle, then substantial, behavior changes.

When we accept that people learn in different ways, we face daily decisions about uniformity and diversity. Teachers have specific expectations for all students. As they make adaptations to accommodate differences in learning style, the distinction between ends and means must be clear. A teacher can state clear learning outcomes and expectations yet diversify the means for reaching those outcomes.

A deep awareness of diverse learning styles also requires a commitment to the belief that all students can be successful learners. If a learning experience is adjusted to accommodate diverse styles, students will be able to use their strengths to achieve this success. We know that not all learning styles are equally valued in schools. Most schools do a more effective job with learners who are reflective, linear, or analytic than those who are active, holistic, personal, or practical. Learners whose styles are accommodated more frequently in school achieve more immediate success. Students who struggle to adapt to an uncomfortable style often underachieve.

When educators work together on goals and objectives for their own programs, a style perspective becomes a common theme. As new curriculum materials are selected, discipline policies formed, and staff development goals set, questions of individual diversity and style will be prominent. The concepts of learning styles will be discussed on a regular basis, and opportunities for learning more about the theories and research will grow from these discussions.

Belief in learning styles becomes a rationale for many educational decisions. It is particularly important for teachers to adapt new techniques through an understanding of learning styles. In other words, a teacher would be motivated to apply a new method with the goal of accommodating the needs of certain students in the classroom. By focusing on learning styles, teachers would understand that a specific technique is successful because it provides the opportunity for approaching a task in a way that is important for certain, though not necessarily all, learners.

For example, cooperative learning is successful not just because it is an alternative to lecture but because it allows some students the opportunity to process externally, to work with their peers, and to share responsibility for a task. Integrated curriculum is successful because it offers opportunities for connections that are made naturally in some students' minds and for the chance to study a topic in depth, which is appreciated by other students. Indeed, educational innovations that have "worked" can trace a relationship to some students' learning patterns.

Teachers who understand learning style differences will strive for intentional variety in their instruction, curriculum, classroom management, and assessment. Administrators who believe in learning styles actively value differences in teaching styles. Curriculum specialists who practice a learning styles approach encourage diverse programs in classrooms, schools, and the district.

Stretching Teaching Styles

One of the most important ways for practitioners to apply learning styles is by recognizing their own personal teaching styles and stretching their style to meet the needs of different learners. To do this, teachers can develop specific strategies that complement their natural teaching approaches. For example, if a teacher has a strong extraverted style, it is likely this trait is reflected in the instructional strategies she uses in the classroom. Acknowledging this, she can consciously work to choose strategies and techniques that would appeal to more introverted learners. She might allow more quiet think time in the classroom or provide a quiet place for students to work. The latter techniques would be more typical for a teacher with an introverted teaching style, who in turn might need to seek strategies to accommodate extraverted learners.

Teachers need not focus on changing their teaching style but on increasing their professional repertoire by intentionally adding techniques and strategies that complement their strengths. A teacher who has a weakness in the visual area can work intentionally to use more visual symbols to illustrate concepts and principles and to add more visual choices in assignments. A teacher who is highly sequential can intentionally offer open-ended time during the day to allow his students the freedom to do things out of a sequential order.

To get ideas for different approaches and strategies, teachers will benefit from working with staff members who have strengths in style areas that they do not. Teachers can work collaboratively behind the scenes by talking with one another about ideas. However, we often seek a person with a similar teaching style to confirm something that we already are doing successfully. To stretch their styles, teachers must seek ideas from successful colleagues who have different approaches. Similarly, team teaching is most effective when the teachers have different teaching styles.

Finally, teachers can learn to style flex by temporarily adapting to a particular student's learning style. For example, when a student asks how many pages a report should be, the student is indicating a need for specific structure. A teacher who has not provided that is often exhibiting a more open-ended or intuitive teaching style and usually has good reason for not including too much structure in the assignment. However, once the student has asked for structure, he or she has voiced a need. This can be fulfilled by giving that student specific guidelines. A teacher need not change the assignment but answer the student's question in a way that makes sense to him or her. The student who needs structure gets an answer, but a student who doesn't want to be tied down won't feel confined by an exact expectation.

As another example, telling a student who is reluctant to work with a group that working together is going to be "fun" often falls on deaf ears. Students who think that group work is fun won't object to the group process in the first place. By looking through the eyes of the objecting student, the teacher can instead refer to the specific purpose of the group structure and the assignment that each member will be expected to fulfill. This will be a much more effective response to the student's learning style.

Intentional Variety

Perhaps the most common way of responding to individual learning style differences is to vary classroom methods, materials, assignments, and assessments. It is important to realize that intentional variety is not as dependent on quantity as it is on quality of choice.

It is frustrating for a student to be told that there are four choices for an assignment only to find out that every one is a linear sequential choice—and that student does not have that particular learning style approach. This often happens because most teachers develop a variety of options within their own styles but find it much harder to develop genuine options for different styles.

Instructional methods are perhaps the most important place to bring intentional variety into the classroom. When a teacher depends on one or two routine ways of presenting lessons, students who do not learn in those ways and do not have the ability to style flex are consistently at a disadvantage. Every teacher can balance direct instruction with exploratory methods, part-to-whole instruction with a whole-to-part approach, kinesthetic strategies with more quiet reflective strategies, and group processes with independent work.

Students will benefit from classrooms that offer variety in teaching materials as well. Reading materials, audiovisuals, computers, manipulatives, programmed learning books, and workbooks are all valuable resources. Different students learn through different resources.

Both curriculum content and curriculum organization can be intentionally varied to accommodate learning style differences. Some students benefit from an in-depth study of a topic that allows them to develop an understanding of general concepts from the specific example. Other students appreciate a breadth of study and like the fast pace of a survey approach. Some students naturally connect concepts and make relationships, and they thrive on an integrated and thematic approach to curriculum. Other students benefit from the clarity of distinctions and like a focused, specific study. Some students focus on practical application and will learn abstract concepts once the application is clear. Other students explore in a seemingly haphazard way, such as working in learning centers, but still develop clear learning through that exploration.

As teachers think of their own general instructional skills, the areas of motivation and questioning are also relevant for style application. Asking questions with a variety of stylistic approaches in mind is a valuable way to accommodate diversity. Some students appreciate the specificity of recall questions while others value the opportunity to present their opinions and describe their personal values. Some students are skilled at documenting their responses and appreciate questions that allow them to do that. Others are stimulated by questions that require a synthesis of ideas and facts. Different stimuli and expectations also motivate students. Some students are motivated by grades and task completion; other students are motivated by the opportunities to work with their peers or adults.

Another practical application is to diversify students' assignments. Teachers can intentionally design assignments to take advantage of different learning style strengths. In this way, students will have an opportunity to take advantage of their own approaches.

One teacher we worked with carefully designed different assignments for a book report. She organized the various options according to one style model and used four different colored index cards for each of the dominant style approaches. For example, making a timeline of the story appealed to the linear learning style and was on a yellow card. All of the yellow cards had a book report choice that used a linear, sequential, and structured approach. All the blue cards were more open-ended; the pink were more personally oriented; and the green were more research oriented. She then allowed students to make choices among the cards without describing the rationale behind the four colors. She found that students began to choose certain colors more frequently for their book reports. Halfway through the school year, she required students to choose an assignment from a card color that they had not previously chosen. This forced all the students to stretch their styles by using a different approach. Throughout the year, she continued to refine the assignments and make them more interesting and sensitive to the different style needs.

Other important areas for intentional variety are assessment, evaluation, and the physical environment. Once teachers have a clear understanding of diversity of learning styles, intentional variety in many aspects of schooling is one of the most important ways of accommodating these differences.

Diagnostic-Prescriptive Teaching

In many cases, identification of a learner's style helps to develop a specific approach to more efficiently and effectively teach that learner. A diagnostic-prescriptive approach to teaching can lead to success for students who have previously experienced failure. Effective diagnostic-prescriptive teaching involves careful collection of diagnostic information using appropriate assessment instruments, substantiated by observation and validation from the person being assessed. Too often, learners, especially those who have not had consistent success, are not really sure what does work for them. For these students, it is important to talk with them about learning styles and to continue to reevaluate the approaches used.

It also assumes knowledge of appropriate prescriptive teaching responses and materials so that the learner's dominant style can be utilized. This kind of careful and thoughtful process is probably most appropriate when a teacher is responsible for only a small group of learners. Many special education teachers successfully develop specific programs to meet the unique needs of each student. It is important, however, to remember that working through strengths is the goal. Too often, remedial help focuses on deficits and the learner experiences limited success.

Using research on styles to design diagnostic-prescriptive teaching programs is sensitive and challenging because it involves the interaction of human nature and intelligence with the concepts, content, and skills being taught in schools. It must be done carefully.

Teach About Style

Knowing that there are a variety of legitimate ways to learn empowers students. In informal and formal ways, teachers can work with students to help them understand these learning style differences.

Informally, every time an assignment or a project is completed, teachers can take time to talk about the variety of ways students approached the work, emphasizing the diversity of approaches rather than talking about right and wrong ways to do the work. Teachers also can solicit students' ideas for learning strategies: How else could the project have been done? What more could we have added? What would you like to try next time? What would help you to do this work better? And feedback on the teaching approach is also useful: What kinds of things did I do that helped you? What in the book helped you? What more did you need? What others ways could we have worked on this assignment?

Students can learn about learning styles in formal ways by taking a learning styles instrument or by using some of the materials available to study styles, such as the booklet *No Sweat! How to Use Your Learning Style to Be a Better Student* (Tobias & Guild, 1986), based on the global/analytic (FD/FI) approaches. Also useful is *Learning Styles, Personal Exploration and Practical Applications: An Introduction to Style for Secondary Students* (Butler, 1995), based on Butler's work. Direct instruction in learning styles increases students' awareness of their own and others' ways of learning. This knowledge carries both power and responsibility. Students who are educated about learning styles become more actively engaged in the process of learning. They are less likely to give up easily when they meet challenges, and they know there is always more than one way to learn. They have seen their peers approach tasks in a variety of ways, and they know that a shift in approach affects the learning success. They are more likely to believe that they can succeed.

Teaching to Specific Style

We know that many students' styles are regularly ignored in the classroom. Active learners, practical learners, global learners, and personal learners have fewer chances in the classroom to learn in ways that take advantage of their style strengths.

Teachers are sometimes frustrated that active learners are not excited about a project planned as a culmination of a study. But their enthusiasm often has been diminished early by required abstract work. One teacher described how she opened a unit on India by giving students a broad overview of the concepts and activities that would be included during the four-week study. The culmination was to be preparing and eating an Indian meal. One boy slammed his book closed and said, "Now you're talking! Let's get on with it!"

In the same way, the practical learner needs the realistic application to be clear early in the learning. Often, teachers tell students about eventual practical uses, but some learners need to experience reality early in the lessons to see that the concepts are useful.

Global learners want to learn "a, b, and c" together, not in isolation. It is often true that they will not be competent in "a" before they go to "b," but the competence develops as they grapple with the whole. A teacher described her frustration trying to learn to juggle piece by piece. She was required to start by raising her hand with a certain rhythm and placement. Then she was given one scarf to use to practice the movement. Finally, in frustration, she blurted out, "Give me all the scarves." The teacher said, "But you'll drop them." Her response was, "But I'll never learn if I can't have them all." And she did, indeed, learn with all three scarves after numerous drops.

Personal learners describe many frustrations in school learning. "What does this mean for me?" is their constant question. When it's not answered, they turn their attention to things they do care about. For them social relations are essential and directly related to learning. When a teacher doesn't remember their names several weeks into the semester, they can't believe that teacher can help them learn.

Ironically, the active, practical, holistic, and personal traits are valued by the work world in our society. Yet we often emphasize just the opposite qualities for success in school. We must make special efforts to accommodate these styles in our schools.

Applications to honor diversity are as varied as the differences of people involved in education. This is not to justify that "anything goes" but to say that sensitive and elegant applications of learning styles are all around us and will continue to evolve.

18

Staff Development and Style

Irvin Feld had found that their talents comple-
mented each other. Kenneth, for example, takes
particular interest in the beginning of a concept.
He has a gift for picturing in his mind how the show
will look on opening night even before the first
rehearsal has been held. Irvin Feld, on the other
hand, looks forward to the final rehearsals—when a
detail can be added, a refinement made, that will
make the highlights of the show really sparkle—the
way a jeweler polishes the facets of a diamond.
This combination of the son who likes to look at the
big picture and the father who pays attention to
the tiniest detail, gives a depth to their productions
that is part of the Feld approach.

–From a Souvenir Program
Ringling Bros. and Barnum & Bailey Circus

All competent educators can identify the various ways they currently
respect individual differences in their work. But how can educators
learn to better work with the diversity of styles adults and students
bring to schools? This chapter discusses how staff development can
help accomplish that goal.

Some applications of style research are systematic and formal, beginning with studying a particular model and then developing and implementing specific strategies to respond to staff and student diversity. Other applications are more informal, with human diversity valued throughout the school in subtle and pervasive ways—and the word *style* seldom used.

Some researchers believe that a serious effort to accommodate differences in style must result in a total restructuring of schools. When diversity of style is accepted and acted upon, education will focus on the dynamic interaction among people, content, and process. Each school's design and reality must reflect that interaction.

What Style Means for Staff Development

The best staff development efforts elicit enthusiasm and excitement from all involved. They offer continuing opportunities for all members of the school community to participate in activities for professional and personal growth. We've seen the concept of style successfully used as an umbrella for a variety of staff development efforts.

Respect for individual differences and diversity implies staff development programs that give substantial decision-making power to staff. Staff members should have a good deal of say over process and content. When we believe that style differences can contribute positively to schools, staff development efforts will be used to encourage individual, personal growth. This concept implies an acceptance of different professional interests and needs based on individual style and ongoing efforts to accommodate and implement what is learned.

Because we have shown throughout this book that style concepts relate to all aspects of the educational process, staff development certainly should include attention to style. Efforts to design, evaluate, or implement curriculum should encompass attention to individual differences. And efforts directed at developing specific instructional skills need to focus on the individual differences of teachers and students. Too often, a school staff will have inservice training on computers on Tuesday, then a learning styles session on Thursday—and never the twain shall meet. No wonder teachers get frustrated!

Most important, formal and informal staff development efforts need to be reinforced every day in a variety of situations. Administrators who offer training on learning styles but then don't encourage diversity among staff members are, of course, defeating their own purposes. Similarly, a one-day presentation on styles without ongoing encouragement and follow-up thwarts the purpose of professional "development."

Style as a Content Topic

As a content topic for staff development, "style" offers the opportunity for professional growth in a number of ways. The concepts of individual style differences have implications for all areas of curriculum and instruction. We previously discussed how the theories of individual style can be used as a basis for building positive communication and interpersonal relationships. These concepts can become a basis for team building and for peer coaching. Concepts of style also can be a basis for encouraging effective communication with parents and with the community at large. They can be a basis for developing positive teacher-student relationships and for encouraging students to interact positively with one another. The climate of a school depends on the ability of all individuals to respect one another and to value one another's diversity. This respect can be furthered through knowledge about style differences and acceptance of the value of diversity.

One school district we work with initially used style to focus on communication and team building among central office staff and building administrators. Then secretaries and support personnel were introduced to basic style concepts and brought together with administrators to strengthen their communication skills and work relationships. "Now I see why you do that!" was a typical comment. Eventually, counselors were included, and school board members and teachers became part of the team focus, too.

Concepts of style differences can become a basis for organizing and managing schools. Studies of individual needs can provide a framework for thinking about organizing the school day, curriculum, class routines and schedule, discipline policies, elective programs, and team teaching. Though consistency in certain policies is necessary in any large organization, respect for individual differences is still a key issue.

For example, when one school district changed from a traditional junior high school structure to the integrated program organization of a middle school, we used concepts of style to help prepare the staff. Teachers examined their own styles in light of their new roles and challenges. They worked with one another in their new teams to plan for making the best use of their individual strengths. They practiced joint curriculum planning and focused on finding ways to accommodate needs of students with diverse styles.

Another content topic for staff development is developing a broad repertoire of teaching strategies and behaviors. When teachers understand their own styles and reflect on the strengths and limitations of those approaches for diverse groups of students, they can identify ways to stretch their teaching patterns. This kind of staff development will be more meaningful when it relates directly to the personal needs, goals, and style of each teacher.

Teachers at one school invited a colleague of ours to help them "stretch" their teaching styles. Working with one model of style, they first developed self-awareness about their teaching styles. They then examined students' learning style needs. Each teacher prepared a personal growth plan identifying goals and actions for trying new teaching behaviors. They worked in subgroups and used peer coaching to implement their plans. A rainbow colored button reading "We Teach With Style" became a proud symbol of their efforts and commitment.

Another school district formed teams of administrators and teachers from each school to study student learning styles. We worked with them to develop their awareness of different aspects of learning style by introducing several research models. Over a few years, individual school teams applied the concepts in different ways. Some focused on curriculum materials, some on teaching methods, and others on student-teacher relationships. One group used information on field-dependent-independent perception to expand the teaching of reading beyond a totally phonic approach. One elementary school designed a bookmark for their reading text listing modality style characteristics as they apply to reading. The teachers use the bookmark as a daily reminder to direct their reading instruction to all modality strengths.

In previous chapters we spoke about evaluation, counseling, study skills, higher-level thinking, technology, and parenting. These can provide specific areas for the application of style for staff development.

How to Use Style

Three steps are necessary to design staff development using concepts of style. First is an awareness and knowledge of the concepts, ideas, and issues. This awareness must be thorough enough that each individual is able to develop a personal understanding of style. This takes time. An introduction to style must be given by someone knowledgeable about style and sincere about celebrating diversity. The person introducing style to others must know the research, understand the complexities and subtleties of the concepts, and be able to model respect for differences.

Once aware of style differences, people must make a personal commitment to respect and honor individual diversity. For many educators this is a reaffirmation of their values and beliefs; for others it's a new challenge. It reminds all of us that it is much easier to accept individual diversity in theory than in practice; it is much easier to say we respect uniqueness than it is to treat all people with that respect!

Once the awareness and personal commitment have been developed, each staff member needs to develop an action plan and ask a fundamental question: What effect will the concepts of style have on my professional behavior? It is at this point that staff members should have some options for applying the information about styles. It is contradictory to espouse a theory of individual style and then require all staff members to apply the theory in exactly the same way. The concepts themselves are better served when staff members individually or as a group develop their own plans for applications. Some people may want to work toward accommodating diversity in curriculum. Others may want to work on their interpersonal relationships and communication with other staff members. Some staff may choose to work on their classroom management and discipline strategies.

This emphasis on individual options does not negate the importance of a school staff working toward a common vision and shared goals. Style becomes important as individual staff members decide how to reach the goals. In much the same way as teachers in the classroom, administrators can hold each staff member accountable for working toward a common school goal but still respect the staff member's unique way of pursuing the goal.

Finally, we have learned much recently about successful staff development. We know that staff development must be supported with appropriate follow-up and resources. We know that it should involve a commitment from all levels of the professional staff. Those planning to use style in staff development efforts must practice what they preach. They must be knowledgeable about styles and committed to the practice of style.

A Final Word

In many ways, the homily of the oyster and the pearl can be used to summarize our attitudes about individual differences in style. Irritations get into an oyster's shell, and the oyster doesn't like them. But when it accepts their reality, it settles down to make one of the most beautiful things in the world: a pearl. When people are fundamentally different from us, it can cause irritations. But these very differences, when appreciated, can be used to benefit all, and the irritations become a catalyst for growth. The study of style should be a positive reminder of the reason most of us chose to become educators: the challenge of helping individuals reach their full potential. The implementation of style is a joyous celebration of diversity!

References

Allport, G. W. (1937/1961). *Pattern and growth in personality.* New York: Holt, Rinehart and Winston. (Original work published 1937)

Armstrong, T. (1987). *In their own way: Discovering and encouraging your child's personal learning style.* Los Angeles: Jeremy P. Tarcher, Inc.

Armstrong, T. (1994). Multiple intelligences in the classroom: Alexandria, VA: ASCD.

Armstrong, T. (1995). *The Myth of the ADD child.* New York: A Dutton Book, Penguin Group.

Armstrong, T. (1996). Labels can last a lifetime. *Learning, 24*(6), 41–43.

Barbe, W. B., & Milone, M. N. (1981). What we know about modality strengths. *Educational Leadership, 38*(5), 378–380.

Barbe, W. B., & Milone, M. N. (1982). Teaching through modality strengths: Look before you leap. In National Association of Secondary School Principals (Ed.), *Student learning styles and brain behavior: Programs, instrumentation, research* (pp. 54–57). Reston, VA: Editor.

Barbe, W. B., & Swassing, R. H. (1979, 1988). *Teaching through modality strengths: Concepts and practices.* Columbus, OH: Zaner-Bloser, Inc. (P.O. Box 16764, Columbus, OH 43216).

Barbe, W. B., & Swassing, R. H. (1979). *The Swassing-Barbe modality index.* Columbus, OH: Zaner-Bloser, Inc. (P.O. Box 16764, Columbus, OH 43216).

Barger, N. J., & Kirby, L. K. (1993). The interaction of cultural values and type development: INTP woman across cultures. *Bulletin of Psychological Type, 16,* 14–16.

Barth, R. S. (1980). *Run school run.* Cambridge, MA: Harvard University Press.

Bennett, C. (1986). *Comprehensive multicultural education, theory and practice.* Boston: Allyn and Bacon.

Berry, J. W. (1979). Culture and cognitive style. In A. Marsella, R. Tharp, & T. Ciborowski (Eds.), *Perspectives on cross-cultural psychology.* San Francisco: Academic Press.

Bert, C. R. G., & Bert, M. (1992). The Native American: An exceptionality in education and counseling. (ERIC Document Reproduction Service No. ED 351 168)

Brandt, R. (1990). On learning styles: A conversation with Pat Guild. *Educational Leadership, 48*(2), 10–13.

Brandt, R. (1997). On using knowledge about our brain: A conversation with Bob Sylwester. *Educational Leadership, 54*(6), 16–19.

Brooks, J. G., & Brooks, M. G. (1993). *In search of understanding: The case for constructivist classrooms.* Alexandria, VA: ASCD.

Butler, K. (1995). *Learning styles, personal exploration and practical applications: An introduction to style for secondary students.* Columbia, CT: The Learners Dimension.

Butler, K. A. (1984). *Learning and teaching style in theory and practice.* Maynard, MA: Gabriel Systems, Inc.

Caine, R. N., & Caine, G. (1991). *Making Connections: Teaching and the human brain.* Alexandria, VA: ASCD.

Caine, R. N., and Caine, G. (1997). *Education on the edge of possibility.* Alexandria, VA: ASCD.

Campbell, B. (1994). *The multiple intelligences handbook: Lesson plans and more.* Standwood, WA: Campbell and Associates, Inc.

Campbell, L., Campbell, B., & Dickinson, D. (1996). *Teaching and learning through multiple intelligences.* Needham Heights, MA: Allyn and Bacon.

Cantor, N. (1946/1972). *Dynamics of learning.* New York: Agathon Press, Inc. (Original work published 1946) (Distributed by Schocken Books, Inc., New York)

Carbo, M. (1981). *Reading style inventory.* Roslyn Heights, NY: Learning Research Associates. (P.O. Box 39, Roslyn Heights, NY 11577)

Carbo, M. (1982, February). Teaching reading the way children learn to read. *Early Years,* 43–46.

Carbo, M. (1997). Reading styles times twenty. *Educational Leadership, 54*(6), 38–42.

Checkley, K. (1997, September). The first seven . . . and the eighth: A conversation with Howard Gardner. *Educational Leadership, 55,* 8–13.

Claxton, C. S. (1990). Learning styles, minority students, and effective education. *Journal of Development Education, 14,* 6–8, 35.

Coates, S. (1972). *Preschool embedded figures test.* Palo Alto, CA: Consulting Psychologists Press, Inc.

Combs, A. W., Avila, D. L. , & Purkey, W. (1971). *Helping relationships: Basic concepts for the helping professions.* Boston: Allyn and Bacon, Inc.

Cornett, C. E. (1983). *What you should know about teaching and learning styles.* Bloomington, IN: Phi Delta Kappa Educational Foundation.

Cox, B., & Ramirez, M., III. (1981). Cognitive styles: Implications for multi-ethnic education. In J. Banks (Ed.), *Education in the 80's.* Washington, DC: National Education Association.

Dunn, R. (1982). Teaching students through their individual learning styles: A research report. In National Association of Secondary School Principals (Ed.), *Student learning styles and brain behavior: Programs, instrumentation, research* (pp. 142–151). Reston, VA: Editor.

Dunn, R. (1997). The goals and track record of multicultural education. *Educational Leadership, 54*(7), 74–77.

Dunn, R., Beaudry, J., & Klavas, A. (1989). Survey of research on learning styles. *Educational Leadership, 46*(6), 50–58.

Dunn, R., Beaudry, J., & Klavas, A. (1995). A meta-analytic validation of the Dunn and Dunn model of learning style preferences. *Journal of Educational Researchers, 88*(6), 353–362.

Dunn, R., & Dunn, K. (1975a). *Educators' self-teaching guide to individualizing instructional programs.* New York: Parker Publishing Company.

Dunn, R., & Dunn, K. (1975b). Finding the best fit: Learning styles, teaching styles. *NASSP Bulletin, 59,* 37–49.

Dunn, R., Dunn, K., & Price, G. E. (1975, 1978 LSI; 1979 PEPS). Learning style inventory and productivity environmental preference survey. Lawrence, KS: Price Systems, Inc. (Box 3067, Lawrence, KS 66046)

Elkind, D. (1981). *The hurried child: Growing up too fast too soon.* Reading, MA: Addison Wesley Publishing Co.

Fogarty, R., & Stoehr, J. (1994). *Integrating curricula with multiple intelligences: Teams, themes, and threads.* Palatine, IL: IRI/Skylight, Inc.

Frankfurter, F. (1949). Dennis v. US, US Report, Vol 339, p. 184.

Gagnon, P. (1995). What should children learn? *The Atlantic Monthly, 276*(6), 65–78.

Gardner, H. (1983). *Frames of mind: The theory of multiple intelligences.* New York: Basic Books.

Gardner, H. (1991). *The unschooled mind: How children think and how schools should teach.* New York: Basic Books.

Gardner, H. (1995). Reflections on multiple intelligences: Myths and messages. *Kappan, 77*(3), 202–209.

Garger, S. (1990). Is there a link between learning style and neurophysiology? *Educational Leadership, 48*(2), 63–65.

Garger, S., & Guild, P. (1984). Learning styles: The crucial differences. *Curriculum Review, 23*(1), 9–12.

Garger, S., & Guild, P. (1985). Schooling: Getting in style with our times. *Context and Conflict, 13*(1), 11–12.

Gilligan, C. (1993). *In a different voice: Psychological theory and women's development.* Boston: Harvard University Press.

Glatthorn, A. A. (1984). *Differentiated supervision.* Alexandria, VA: ASCD.

Golay, K. (1982). *Learning patterns and temperament styles.* Newport Beach, CA: Mana-Systems.

Goleman, D. (1995). *Emotional intelligence: Why it can matter more than IQ.* New York: Bantam Books.

Goodlad, J. I. (1984). *A place called school: Prospects for the future.* New York: McGraw Hill Book Company.

Grady, M. P. (1990). *Whole brain education.* Fastback #301. Bloomington, IN: Phi Delta Kappa Educational Foundation.

Gregorc, A. F. (1982a). *An adult's guide to style.* Maynard, MA: Gabriel Systems, Inc. (P.O. Box 357, Maynard, MASS. 01754)

Gregorc, A. F. (1982b). *Gregorc style delineator: Developmental, technical, and administration manual* (Rev. ed.). Maynard, MA: Gabriel Systems, Inc. (P.O. Box 357, Maynard, MASS. 01754)

Guild, P. (1982). Learning styles: Understanding before action. *Context and Conflict, 10,* 4–6.

Guild, P. (1984, June). Different gifts in learning. *Parish Teacher, 7*(10), 6.

Guild, P. (1989, August). Meeting students' learning styles. *Instructor, 1,* 14–17.

Guild, P. (1992). Learning to teach by teaching for learning. *Curriculum in Context, 20*(1), 26–27. (Reprinted from *Curriculum in Context, 15*(2), 18–19).

Guild, P. (1994a). The culture/learning style connection. *Educational Leadership, 51*(8), 16–21.

Guild, P. (1994b). Making sense of learning styles: Addressing student differences in the classroom links directly to leadership and management styles. *The School Administrator, 51*(1), 8–13.

Guild, P. B. (1980). Learning styles: Knowledge, issues and applications for classroom teachers. Unpublished doctoral dissertation, University of Massachusetts, Amherst.

Guild, P. B. (1987). How leaders' minds work. In L. Sheive & M. Schoenbreit (Eds.), *Leadership: Examining the elusive/1987 ASCD yearbook* (pp. 81–92). Alexandria, VA: ASCD.

Guild, P. B. (1997). Where do the learning theories overlap? *Educational Leadership, 55*(1), 30–31.

Guild, P., McKinney, L., & Fouts, J. (1990). *A study of the learning styles of elementary students: Low achievers, average achievers, high achievers.* Seattle, WA: The Teaching Advisory. (P.O. Box 99131, Seattle, WA 98199)

Hale-Benson, J. E. (1986). *Black children: Their roots, culture, and learning styles* (Rev. ed.). Baltimore: Johns Hopkins University Press.

Hatch, T. (1997). Getting specific about multiple intelligences. *Educational Leadership, 54*(6), 26–29.

Hilliard, A. G., III. (1989, January). Teachers and cultural styles in a pluralistic society. *NEA Today, 65–69.*

Hoffman, J. L., & Betkouski, M. (1981). A summary of Myers-Briggs type indicator research applications in education. In T. G. Carskadon (Ed.), *Research in Psychological Type 3* (pp. 3–41). Mississippi State, MS: Mississippi State University Press.

Hunter, M. (1979). Diagnostic teaching. *The Elementary School Journal, 80,* 41–46.

Irvine, J. J., & York, D. E. (1995). Learning styles and culturally diverse students: A literature review. In J. A. Banks & C. A. Banks (Eds.), *Handbook of research on multicultural education.* New York: Macmillian.

James, W. (1890/1981). *The principles of psychology* (Vol. 1). Boston: Harvard University Press. (Original work published 1890)

Joyce, B. R., Hersh, R. H., & McKibbin, M. (1983). *The structure of school improvement.* New York: Longman.

Jung, C. G. (1921/1971). *Psychological types.* Princeton, NJ: Princeton University Press. (Original work published 1921)

Kagan, J. (1966). Reflection impulsivity: The generality and dynamics of conceptual tempo. *Journal of Abnormal Psychology, 71*(1), 17–24.

Karp, S. A., & Konstadt, N. (1971). *Children's embedded figures test.* Palo Alto, CA: Consulting Psychologists Press, Inc.

Keefe, J. W. (1982). Foreword. In National Association of Secondary School Principals (Ed.), *Student learning styles and brain behavior programs, instrumentation, research.* Reston, VA: Editor.

Keirsey, D., & Bates, M. (1978). *Please understand me: Character and temperament types.* Del Mar, CA: Prometheus, Nemesis.

Klein, G. S. (1951). The personal world through perception. In R. R. Blake & G. V. Ramsey (Eds.), *Perception: An approach to personality* (pp. 328–355). New York: Ronald Press.

Kohn, A. (1993). *Punished by rewards: The trouble with gold stars, incentive plans, A's, praise, and other bribes.* New York: Houghton Mifflin.

Kolb, D. (1976). *Learning style inventory.* Boston: McBer & Company. (137 Newberry St., Boston, MA 02116)

Kuhn, T. S. (1961/1970). *The structure of scientific revolutions* (2nd ed.). Chicago: University of Chicago Press. (Original worked published 1961)

Kusler, G. E. (1982). Getting to know you. In National Association of Secondary School Principals (Ed.), *Student learning styles and brain behavior: Programs, instrumentation, research* (pp. 11–14). Reston, VA: Editor.

Latham, A. (1997). Responding to cultural learning styles. *Educational Leadership, 54*(7), 88–89.

Lawrence, G. (1979/1982/1993). *People types and tiger stripes: A practical guide to learning styles* (3rd ed.). Gainesville, FL: Center for Applications of Psychological Type, Inc. (Original work published 1979) (Learning Styles Network, School of Education and Human Services, St. John's University, Grand Central and Utopia Parkways, Jamaica, NY 11439)

Lazear, D. (1994). *Multiple intellegences approaches to assessment: Solving the assessment conundrum.* Tucson, AZ: Zephyr Press.

Letteri, C. A. (1980). Cognitive profile: Basic determinant of academic achievement. *The Journal of Educational Research, 73*(4), 195–198.

Lowenfeld, V. (1945). Tests for visual and haptical aptitudes. *American Journal of Psychology, 58*(1), 100–111.

Mackenzie, D. E. (1983). Research for school improvement: An appraisal of some recent trends. *Educational Researcher, 12*(4), 5–17.

May, R. (Ed.). (1969). *Existential psychology* (2nd ed.). New York: Random House.

May, R., Angel, E., & Ellenberger, H. F. (Eds.). (1958). Existence, a new discussion in psychiatry and psychology. New York: Simon and Schuster.

McCarthy, B. (1980). *The 4MAT System: Teaching to learning styles with right/left mode techniques.* Barrington, IL: Excel, Inc.

McCarthy, B. (1985). What 4MAT training teaches us about staff development. *Educational Leadership, 42*(7), 61–68.

McCarthy, B. (1997). A tale of four learners: 4MAT's learning styles. *Educational Leadership, 54*(6), 46–51.

McCarthy, B., & Leflar, S. (Eds.). (1983). *4MAT in action: Creative lesson plans for teaching to learning styles with right/left mode techniques.* Barrington, IL: Excel.

McCaulley, M. H., & Natter, F. L. (1974/1980). *Psychological (Myers-Briggs) type differences in education* (2nd ed.). Gainesville, FL: Center For Applications of Psychological Type, Inc. (Original work published 1974)

Meisgeier, C., & Murphy, E. (1987). Murphy-Meisgeier type indicator for children. Palo Alto, CA: Consulting Psychologist Press.

Milone, M. N., Jr. (1980). Modality and the kindergarten child. In *Zaner-Bloser kindergarten resource book* (p. xiii). Columbus: Zaner-Bloser, Inc.

Mok, P. P. (1975). *Communicating styles survey.* Dallas, TX: Training Associates Press. (1177 Rockingham, Richardson, TX 75080)

Moore, A. J. (1990). Learning styles of Native Americans and Asians. Paper presented at the Annual Meeting of the American Psychological Association, Boston. (ERIC Document Reproduction Service No. ED 330 535)

Myers, I. B. (1962). *Introduction to type.* Palo Alto, CA: Consulting Psychologists Press, Inc.

Myers, I. B. (1980). Taking type into account in education. In M. H. McCauley & F. L. Natter, *Psychological (Myers-Briggs) type differences in education*. (2nd ed.). Gainesville, FL: Center for Applications of Psychological Type, Inc. (Original work published 1974)

Myers, I. B. (1990). *Gifts differing* (2nd ed.). Palo Alto, CA: Consulting Psychologists Press, Inc.

Myers, I. B., & Briggs, K. C. (1943/1976). *Myers-Briggs Type Indicator*. Palo Alto, CA: Consulting Psychologists Press, Inc. (Original work published 1943) (577 College Ave., Palo Alto, CA 94306)

Oltman, P. K., Raskin, E., & Witkin, H. A. (1971). *Group embedded figures test*. Palo Alto, CA: Consulting Psychologists Press, Inc.

Peters, T. J., & Waterman, R., Jr. (1982). *In search of excellence*. New York: Harper & Row.

Ramirez, M., III. (1989). Pluralistic education: A bicognitive-multicultural model. *The Clearinghouse Bulletin, 3*, 4–5.

Ramirez, M., & Castaneda, A. (1974). *Cultural democracy, bicognitive development and education*. New York: Academic Press.

Restak, R. M. (1972). *The brain: The last frontier*. New York: Doubleday and Company.

Roszak, T. (1972). *Where the wasteland ends: Politics and transcendence in postindustrial society*. New York: Doubleday and Company, Inc.

Rutter, M., Maughan, B., Motimore, P., & Ouston, J., (with Smith, A.). (1979). Fifteen thousand hours: Secondary schools and their effects on children. Cambridge, MA: Harvard University Press.

Samples, B., Hammond, B., & McCarthy, B. (1985). *4MAT and science: Toward wholeness in science education*. Barrington, IL: Excel.

Shade, B. J. (1989). The influence of perceptual development on cognitive style: Cross ethnic comparisons. *Early Child Development and Care, 51*, 137–155.

Shor, I. (1992). *Empowering education: Critical teaching for social change*. Chicago: The University of Chicago Press.

Silver, H., Strong, R., & Perini, M. (1997). Integrating learning styles and multiple intelligences. *Educational Leadership, 55*(1), 22–27.

Simon, A., & Byram, C. (1977). *You've got to reach 'em to teach 'em*. Dallas, TX: Training Associates Press.

Sizer, T. R. (1984). *Horace's compromise: The dilemma of the American high school*. Boston: Houghton Mifflin Company.

Sylwester, R. (1995). *A celebration of neurons: An educator's guide to the human brain*. Alexandria, VA: ASCD.

Tobias, C., & Guild, P. (1986). *No sweat! How to use your learning style to be a better student*. Seattle: The Teaching Advisory. (P.O. Box 99131, Seattle, WA 98199)

Toffler, A. (1981). *The third wave*. New York: Bantam Books.

Tyler, L. E. (1965). *The psychology of human differences* (3rd ed.). New York: Appleton Century Crofts.

Vasquez, J. A. (1991). Cognitive style and academic achievement. In J. Lynch, C. Modgil, & S. Modgil (Eds.), *Cultural diversity and the schools: Consensus and controversy*. London: Falconer Press.

Walker, D. E. (1980). A barnstorming tour of writing on curriculum. In A. W. Foshay (Ed.), *Considered action for curriculum improvement, 1980 ASCD Yearbook* (pp. 71–81). Alexandria, VA: ASCD.

Wickes, F. G. (1927/1966). *The inner world of childhood*. Englewood Cliffs, NJ: Prentice Hall, Inc. (Original work published 1927)

Witkin, H. A. (1969). Embedded figures test. Palo Alto, CA: Consulting Psychologists Press, Inc. (577 College Ave., Palo Alto, CA 94306)

Witkin, H., & Goodenough, O. (1981). Cognitive styles: Essence and origins. New York: International Universities Press, Inc. (Available from Consulting Psychologists Press, Inc.)

Witkin, H. A., Moore, C. A., Goodenough, D. R., & Cox, P. W. (1977). Field-dependent and field-independent cognitive styles and their educational implications. *Review of Educational Research, 47,* 1–64.

Witkin, H. A., Oltman, P. K., Cox, P. W., Ehrlichman, E., Hamm, R. M., & Ringler, R. W. (1973). *Field-dependence-independence and psychological differentiation: A bibliography*. Princeton, NJ: Educational Testing Service. (Supplements 1–5, 1974–1981; also available from Consulting Psychologists Press, Inc.)

Yalom, I. D. (1980). *Existential psychotherapy*. New York: Basic Books.

Annotated Bibliography

Armstrong, T. (1987). *In their own way: Discovering and encouraging your child's personal learning style.* Los Angeles: Jeremy P. Tarcher, Inc. (distributed by St. Martin's Press, NY).

Based on the multiple intelligence framework, this book gives parents information and suggestions for working with their unique children.

Armstrong, T. (1994). *Multiple intelligences in the classroom.* Alexandria, VA: ASCD.

Presents foundations of multiple intelligences with practical applications for the classroom.

ASCD. *Educational Leadership 36* (January 1979), *48* (October 1990), *55* (September 1997).

The 1979 and 1990 issues are devoted to learning styles. The 1997 issue covers multiple intelligences. Articles by researchers and practitioners.

ASCD. (1993). *Teaching to learning styles.* Alexandria, VA: Author.

Pat Guild was design and content consultant for this video program showing teachers in elementary, middle, and high schools applying learning style concepts. The video won the CINE Golden Eagle Award, the Silver Screen Award at the U.S. International Film and Video Festival, and the Bronze Apple Award from the National Educational Film and Video Festival.

Barbe, W. B. (1985). *Growing up learning.* Washington, DC: Acropolis Books Ltd. (Colortone Building, 2400 - 17th St., N.W., Washington, DC 20009).

Written for parents, discusses children's modality strengths and gives suggestions for home and school.

Barbe, W. B., & Swassing, R. H. (1994). *Teaching through modality strengths: Concepts and practices.* Columbus, OH: Zaner-Bloser, Inc.

Defines modality, reviews the history of modality based instruction, describes ways to identify modality strengths, and offers practical suggestions for instruction.

Bargar, J. R., Bargar, R. R., & Cano, J. M. (1994). *Discovering learning preferences and learning differences in the classroom.* Columbus, OH: Ohio Agricultural Education Curriculum Materials Service. (The Ohio State University, 2120 Fyffe Rd., Columbus, Ohio 43210)

A practical book applying Jung's theory to the classroom by identifying students' preferences and appropriate teaching strategies.

Barth, R. S. (1980). *Run school run.* Cambridge, MA: Harvard University Press.
A public school principal's story of creating a school that builds upon diversity among students, teachers, and parents. A how-to book that describes organizational decisions that value diversity rather than uniformity.

Becher, P., Bledsoe, L., & Mok, P. (1977). *The strategic woman.* Dallas, TX: Training Associates Press. (1177 Rockingham, Richardson, TX 75080)
Based on the four personality types described by Carl Jung, this book focuses on personal growth and strategies for interpersonal relationships.

Bennett, C. *Comprehensive multicultural education, theory and practice.* 2nd Edition. (1990). Boston: Allyn and Bacon.
This clear and comprehensive book has an excellent section on learning styles and threads the concept of learning styles throughout its presentation of theory. Offers suggestions for practice.

Bolton, R., & Boston, D. G. (1984). *Social style/management style.* New York: American Management Associations. (135 West 50th St., New York, NY 10020)
Identifies four social styles based on the work of David Merrill and Roger Reid. Discusses self-awareness and applying style to interpersonal relationships, careers, goal setting, and management.

Butler, K. A. (1988). *It's all in your mind: A student's guide to style.* Columbia, CT: The Learner's Dimension. (Box 6, Columbia, CT 06237)
An introduction to Gregorc's learning style model for students with suggestions for each style to study effectively and be versatile.

Butler, K. A. (1984, revised 1987). *Learning and teaching style in theory and practice* (2nd ed.). Columbia, CT: The Learner's Dimension. (Box 6, Columbia, CT 06237)
Based on Gregorc's style model, this book presents the concept of style with extensive examples in learning and teaching. It offers practical, detailed suggestions for using style in instruction and curriculum.

Caine, R. N., & Caine, G. (1991). *Making connections: Teaching and the human brain.* Alexandria, VA: ASCD.
A presentation of facts and theories about the human brain including 12 principles and implications for schooling.

Caine, R. N., & Caine, G. (1997). *Education on the edge of possibility.* Alexandria, VA: ASCD.
A description of the Caines' application of brain-based learning set in the context of larger issues of educational beliefs and practices.

Campbell, L., Campbell, B., & Dickinson, D. (1996). *Teaching and learning through multiple intelligences.* Needham Heights, MA: Allyn and Bacon.
An overview of multiple intelligences theory with practical suggestions for teaching through each intelligence.

Carbo, M., Dunn, R., & Dunn, K. (1986). *Teaching students to read through their individual learning styles.* Englewood Cliffs, NJ: Prentice Hall.

Describes Dunn and Dunn's model of styles and Carbo's application to reading, with extensive examples of adapting reading materials to meet students' learning styles.

Claxton, C. S., & Ralston, Y. (1978*). Learning styles: Their impact on teaching and administration.* Washington, DC: American Association for Higher Education.
The first part gives a good overview of the research on cognitive styles. Written for application at the college level.

Cornett, C. E. (1983). *What you should know about teaching and learning styles.* Bloomington, IN: Phi Delta Kappa Educational Foundation.
An overview of learning styles, drawing the relationship to teaching styles and brain research. Includes a detailed list of assessment instruments and suggestions for accommodating learning styles.

Dunn, R., & Dunn, K. (1978). *Teaching students through their individual learning styles: A practical approach.* Reston, VA: Reston Publishing Co., Inc.
Describes detailed classroom activities and lessons that respond to various student learning styles as defined by the Dunns' 18 elements.

Entwistle, N. (1981). *Styles of learning and teaching.* New York: John Wiley & Sons.
An integrated outline of important aspects of educational psychology focusing on the processes of learning and teaching and how people differ in their approaches.

Fogarty, R., & Stoehr, J. (1995). *Integrating curriculum with multiple intelligences.* Palatine, IL: IRI/Skylight Publishing, Inc.
Incorporating multiple intelligence theories and the Caines' brain-based education principles, this book gives practical strategies for curriculum.

Gardner, H. (1983). *Frames of mind: The theory of multiple intelligences.* New York: Basic Books.
Identifies and describes the theory of multiple intelligences.

Gardner, H. (1991). *The unschooled mind: How children think and how schools should teach.* New York: Basic Books, A Division of Harper Collins Publishers.
Gardner addresses learning challenges and the importance of multiple perspectives to encourage more depth in education and promotion of success for more students.

Garger, S. (1982). Learning styles: A state of the art and a curriculum design for application. Doctoral dissertation, Seattle University. (Available from University Microfilms International, Ann Arbor, Michigan)
A review of the literature on styles and a description of a curriculum project implementing styles in the counseling department at a high school.

Golay, K. (1982). *Learning patterns and temperament styles.* Newport Beach, CA: Manas Systems. (P.O. Box 106, Newport Beach, CA 92663)

Based on Keirsey's work with Jung's theories and Myers-Briggs definitions, this book profiles four types of learners and offers specific suggestions for accommodating styles through the physical environment, tasks, subject interests, and classroom climate.

Goldstein, K., & Blackman, S. (1978). *Cognitive style, five approaches and relevant research*. New York: John Wiley & Sons.
Addressed to behavioral scientists, this book reviews various approaches to the study of cognitive style. It cites extensive research and theories.

Goleman, D. (1995). *Emotional intelligence: Why it can matter more than IQ*. New York: Bantam Books.
A description of emotional intelligence with a variety of implications, including education.

Grady, M. P. (1990). *Whole brain education* (Fastback No. 301). Bloomington, IN: Phi Delta Kappa Educational Foundation.
This brief introduction to brain research sets a context for the importance of understanding the brain and identifies educational strategies, particularly for visual learners.

Gregorc, A. F. (1982). *An adult's guide to style*. Maynard, MA: Gabriel Systems, Inc. (P.O. Box 357, Maynard, MA 01754)
An overview of Gregorc's style work with an emphasis on self-awareness, acceptance of others' styles, and development of abilities to stretch and flex one's style.

Gregorc, A. F. (1987). *Inside styles: Beyond the basics*. Maynard, MA: Gabriel Systems, Inc. (P.O. Box 357, Maynard, MA 01754)
Gregorc responds to questions about his research, expanding and enlarging his view of style and its meaning for student and teacher, therapist and patient, administrator and faculty, supervisor and employee.

Guild, P. (1995). *An overview of learning styles*. Alexandria, VA: ASCD.
A professional development program on tape. Includes six tapes and a self-study guide.

Guild, P., & Hand, K. (1998). *Learning styles: Accommodating students' diverse needs*. Alexandria, VA: ASCD.
A professional development study kit with video excerpts and readings.

Guild, P. O. B. (1980). Learning styles: Knowledge, issues and applications for classroom teachers. Doctoral dissertation, University of Massachusetts. (Available from University Microfilms International, Ann Arbor, Michigan, #80-19, 462.)
An overview of the literature on learning styles leading to generalizations for teachers and some suggested directions for classroom accommodation.

Hanson, J. R., & Silver, H. E. (1982/1996). *Learning styles and strategies*. Morristown, NJ: Silver, Strong and Associates, Inc. (34 Washington Rd., Princeton Junction, NJ 08550), and The Whole Child Press, J. Robert Hanson Associates (Aspen Corporate Park, 1480 Rt. 9, Woodbridge, NJ 07095).
Describes the Hanson-Silver model of learning styles, based on Jung's theory, and gives practical suggestions for the classroom.

Harrison, A. E., & Bramson, R. M. (1982/1996). *Styles of thinking, strategies for asking questions, making decisions, and solving problems.* Garden City, NY: Anchor Press/Doubleday.

Addressed to a business audience, this book describes five Styles of Thinking originally identified by C. West Churchman and Ian Mitroff. It discusses ways to use strengths and to extend personal thinking strategies.

Jung, C. G. (1921/1971). *Psychological types.* Princeton, NJ.: Princeton University Press. (Original work published 1921)

A thorough description of Jung's theory of psychological types.

Keefe, J. W. (1987). *Learning style theory and practice.* Reston, VA: National Association of Secondary School Principals.

A summary of Keefe's review of cognitive, affective, and physiological models of learning styles, with information on brain behavior and application.

Keirsey, D., & Bates, M. (1978). *Please understand me, character and temperament types.* Del Mar, CA: Prometheus, Nemesis. (P.O. Box 2082, Del Mar, CA 92014)

Based on the 16 Myers-Briggs types, this book proposes four temperament types and offers general examples of type in everyday life as well as in teaching and learning.

Kirby, P. (1979). *Cognitive style, learning style and transfer skill acquisition.* Columbus, OH: The National Center for Research in Vocational Education, The Ohio State University. (1960 Kenny Road, Columbus, OH 43210)

Links cognitive and learning style research and theory to the world of work, focusing on the understanding of and ability to use transfer skills and cognitive/learning styles.

Lawrence, G. (1979/1982/1993). *People types and tiger stripes, a practical guide to learning styles.* Gainesville, FL: Center for Applications of Psychological Type, Inc. (2720 N.W Sixth St., Gainesville, FL 32601)

Based on the Myers-Briggs descriptions of 16 types, this expanded revision gives an overview of style and many practical suggestions for instruction, meeting students' developmental needs, considering teaching styles, and organizing staff development programs on styles.

Littauer, F. (1983). *Personality plus.* Old Tappan, NJ: Fleming H. Revell Company.

Using the terms Sanguine, Choleric, Melancholy, and Phlegmatic established by Hippocrates, this book emphasizes building on one's strengths and improving relations with others.

Mamchur, C. (1984). *Insights, understanding yourself and others.* Toronto, Ontario: The Ontario Institute for Studies in Education. (252 Bloor St. West, Toronto, Ontario M5S 1V6)

An exploration of the world of psychological types, based on Carl Jung's concepts. Uses stories, photographs, paintings, and dramatic vignettes to discuss the full potential of the human spirit.

Mamchur, C. (1996). *A teacher's guide to cognitive type theory and learning style.* Alexandria, VA: ASCD.

An overview of Carl Jung's theory of psychological type with applications for teachers.

May, R., Angel, E., & Ellenberger, H. F. (Eds.). (1958). *Existence, a new dimension in psychiatry and psychology.* New York: Simon and Schuster.
A good, readable explanation of existentialism and the existential approach to therapy.

McCarthy, B. (1987). *The 4MAT system: Teaching to learning styles with right/left mode techniques.* Barrington, IL: Excel, Inc. (200 West Station St., Barrington, IL 60010)
A model for teaching based on Kolb's experiential-learning cycle. Includes a variety of sample lessons.

McCarthy, B. (1997). *About learning.* Barrington, IL: Excel, Inc. (200 West Station St., Barrington, IL 60010)
Explanation of learning differences focusing on McCarthy's 4MAT system in content of essential issues about learning.

Meisgeier, C., & Meisgeier, C. (1989). *A parent's guide to type: Individual differences at home and in school.* Palo Alto, CA: Consulting Psychologist Press.
A practical booklet explaining Jung's types with examples in parent-child relationships.

Meisgeier, C., Murphy, E., & Meisgeier, C. (1989). *A teacher's guide to type: A new perspective on individual differences in the classroom.* Palo Alto: CA: Consulting Psychologist Press.
A practical booklet illustrating how teachers can use Jung's theories of type differences to enhance instruction.

Merrill, D., & Reid, R. (1981). *Personal styles and effective performance.* Radnor, PA: Chilton Book Company.
Approached from the perspective of observing social behavior, this book describes styles with extensive examples from business. A good section on versatility.

Milgram, R. M., Dunn, R., & Price, G. E. (Eds.). (1993). *Teaching and counseling gifted and talented adolescents.* Wesport, CT: Praeger Publishers.
An overview of giftedness and the Dunn model of learning style, followed by information about learning styles of gifted and talented learners in several countries.

Murphy, E. (1992). *The developing child: Using Jungian type to understand children.* Palo Alto, CA: Consulting Psychologist Press.
Describes various children's behaviors representative of different types and suggests applications to parenting, building relationships, and teaching.

Myers, I. B. (1962). *Introduction to type.* Palo Alto, CA: Consulting Psychologists Press. (577 College Ave., Palo Alto, CA 94306)
A comprehensive booklet describing the Myers-Briggs types and Jung's original type work.

Myers, I. B. (1980). *Gifts differing*. Palo Alto, CA: Consulting Psychologists Press. (577 College Ave., Palo Alto, CA 94306)

An overview of the Myers-Briggs descriptions of 16 types based on Carl Jung's work on psychological types. Emphasis on the effect of type on personality and human development. Brief section on learning styles.

National Association of Secondary School Principals. (Eds.). (1982). *Student learning styles and brain behavior: Programs, instrumentation, research.* Reston, VA: National Association of Secondary School Principals. (1904 Association Dr., Reston, VA 22091)

A collection of articles from a major NASSP conference on learning styles and brain research. Focuses on programs, research, instrumentation, and applications.

National Association of Secondary School Principals. (Eds.). (1993). *Student learning styles: Diagnosing and prescribing programs.* Reston, VA: National Association of Secondary School Principals. (1904 Association Dr., Reston, VA 22091)

A collection of articles on learning styles by several major researchers in the field.

Neff, L. (1988). *One of a kind: Making the most of your child's uniqueness.* Portland, OR: Multnomah Press.

A practical book for parents and teachers with applications for communication, relationships, and discipline at home and in school. Based on Jung's theories.

Prewitt, B. W., with **Butler, K. A.** (1993). *Learning styles and performance assessment.* Columbia, CT: The Learner's Dimension.

A practical guide to assessment with styles based on Butler and Gregorc's model. Includes reference to multiple intelligences.

Samples, B., Hammond, B., & McCarthy, B. (1980). *4MAT and science: Toward wholeness in science education.* Barrington IL: Excel, Inc. (Box 706, Barrington, IL 60010)

Demonstrates how 4MAT applies to the teaching of science, addresses trends in science education, and includes lesson plans.

Sheive, L. T., & Schoenheit, M. B. (1987). *Leadership: Examining the elusive.* 1987 ASCD Yearbook. Alexandria, VA: ASCD.

Includes references to diversity of styles among educational leaders and a chapter on leadership styles by Pat Guild.

Simon, A., & Byram, C. (1977). *You've got to reach 'em to teach 'em.* Dallas, TX: Training Associates Press. (1177 Rockingham, Richardson, TX 75080)

Based on four communicating styles identified by Carl Jung and described by Paul Mok, this book gives an overview of styles and their implications for teaching and learning. It offers many practical suggestions for teachers, especially for style flexing.

Sylwester, R. (1995). *A celebration of neurons: An educator's guide to the human brain.* Alexandria, VA: ASCD.

This book is an excellent overview of brain research presented in a readable, engaging, and practical way for educators.

Tobias, C. U., & Guild, P. (1985). *No sweat! How to use your learning style to be a better student.* Seattle: The Teaching Advisory. (P.O. Box 99131, Seattle, WA 98199)

A booklet written for students to help them identify their own best ways of learning and use their learning style effectively in school. Includes suggestions for studying effectively, ways to approach particular assignments, and ways to get help from teachers and parents.

Tyler, L. E. (1965). *The psychology of human differences.* (3rd ed.). New York: Appleton Century-Crofts.

A comprehensive text on individual differences describing some factors that produce these differences.

Wickes, F. G. (1927/1966). *The inner world of childhood.* Englewood Cliffs, NJ: Prentice Hall, Inc. (Original work published in 1927)

A sensitive exploration of the intricacies within a parent-child relationship by a Jungian-trained child psychologist. One chapter focuses directly on psychological types.

Witkin, H., & Goodenough, D. R. (1981). *Cognitive styles: essence and origins.* New York: International Universities Press, Inc. (Available from Consulting Psychologists Press, Inc., 577 College Ave., Palo Alto, CA 94306)

Covers the historical development of field dependence-independence and psychological differentiation and the origins of cognitive styles. Summarizes and cites extensive research.

Index

Page numbers followed by "*f*" refer to figures.

About the Authors

Pat Burke Guild is the owner of Pat Guild Associates in Seattle, Washington. This organization trains administrators, teachers, parents, and people in business and other professions to use personal diversity productively in communication, team building, management, teaching, and learning. She is a full-time faculty member of Woodring College of Education at Western Washington University. She has been coordinator of Learning Style Programs at Seattle Pacific University; Director of Education at Antioch University, Seattle; Visiting Faculty at United States International University, Nairobi, Kenya; and an adjunct faculty member of several other universities. She has worked in teacher education and staff development for more than 25 years, was an elementary school principal in Massachusetts, and was a teacher in New York City and Connecticut. She earned her doctorate in International Education and Teacher Education at the University of Massachusetts in 1980. Her dissertation is titled "Learning Styles: Knowledge, Issues and Applications for Classroom Teachers." She can be reached at Box 99131, Seattle, WA 98199, 206-282-3420 (phone and fax) and patguild@isomedia.com (e-mail).

Stephen Garger is Associate Professor and Director of Teacher Education/Chair, Department of Teacher Education at Marist College. He has been a high school teacher, counselor, coach, and administrator in New York City; Missoula, Montana; and Seattle and Issaquah, Washington; and a faculty member at Central College of Iowa, the University of Portland (Oregon) and Education Department Chair at Trinity College of Vermont. Steve has conducted numerous learning styles sessions throughout the United States as well as in Canada and Mexico. He earned his doctorate in Educational Leadership at Seattle University in 1982. His dissertation is titled "Learning Styles: A State of the Art and a Curriculum Design for Application." Garger can be reached at Marist College, Department of Teacher Education, 290 North Rd., Poughkeepsie, NY 12601-1387 USA; 914-575-3000 (phone) and jshc@maristb.marist.edu (e-mail).